A Series of
Surrenders

A MEMOIR OF GRIEF

Debra Lynne Driscoll

A Series of Surrenders

A Memoir of Grief

Paperback Edition
ISBN: 978-0-578-60106-9

Also available in ePub and Kindle formats

Cover design: Steph Houle
Interior layout: Lighthouse24

For my son Sage, my father Colin,
and my first love Nick.

Thank you for the love and the lessons.

In Love and Light, Debra

Contents

Introduction

The Compass.
The tool that holds a direction and points the way forward
and home.

The Moon.
The light in the dark that teaches of cycles, change, and the
never-ending story of letting go and beginning again.

The Elements.
In equal balance they build form and foundation of our
earthbound experience.

"I'VE STUDIED GRIEF," she said to me. "It comes in waves."

I had pulled my car over to the side of the road to listen to my friend. I knew of the waves she was referring to, and I knew she was warning me of the moment they would crash to shore.

"It comes in waves as that is what is needed. The emotional intensity causes chemical processes in the body that allow it to fall and crash. The body seeks balance and will let the waves hit the shore and eventually stop. The intensity is too much to cope with over and over again as the waves crash, so it slows it all down."

The surrender comes in allowing the waves to crash and allowing yourself to recover. They come more than once – the crash and the recovery. Earthbound and alive we seek ground, direction, and light, to see our way forward. As I sit on the shore, wade in the water, and tumble under waves, I seek my bearings through my inner compass, the phases of the moon, and elements that work within me and are of the earth.

DEATH COMES BEARING GIFTS. I remember thinking this so strange when I first learned of the idea as a young twenty-year-old learning tarot. The gifts can be the new beginning beyond letting go, the potential of a changed life, or a fresh start. It is the lesson of the Death card – or at least the lesson I tended to lean into.

Hades, the dark god of the underworld, the lord of death, is the mythical character of the card. Images of Hades show a tall figure dressed in black wearing a helmet. When he emerged into the daylight world his helmet would make him invisible to mortals thus adding to his fear-provoking presence – you never knew when he was close. The mythical Greeks believed the rites of death required a gold coin to be placed in the mouth of the corpse as an offering to Hades. Without the gifted gold coin, it was feared the soul was doomed to wander forever on the shores of the River Styx, one of the four rivers which border the underworld kingdom.

As a twenty-year old, I thought little of death or an underworld, but I did spend time wondering about invisible magic, psychic energy, and what life was really about. Most of my musing was with friends in the living room at our share house in inner-city Brisbane, Queensland. Our small home on Federal St (known to us as Feral St) was often filled with friends and classmates from the university we attended a short walk away. We, as a pack of young ferals, were all wondering about something, were still hopeful, and interested mostly in ourselves. For most of us, it was our first real chance to define ourselves in the way we wanted, not as our family had taught, or what we followed in our peer group at school. For me, this meant an exploration of the spirit world and all its magic. It was my first choice of discovery after my teenage abandonment of the Catholic church.

I grew up in a family that on Sundays went to church. We dressed well but not too fancy, and each weekend would make our way to our local church that for me spelled boredom and the waiting out of the long minutes until the better part of Sunday: the post-church brunch of delicious pastries and the once a week cup of coffee. I often spent time at church either daydreaming or chasing a younger sibling. As the middle child of seven, my younger sisters were a great distraction from the prayers and amens that I was not interested in.

When I was perhaps ten or eleven I realized that if I lay very still and pretended I was asleep on a Sunday morning I would momentarily be forgotten in the commotion of the pre-church dressing and gathering, and would eventually be roused by a sister or my brother. If I lay still and did not dare open my eyes I would create lateness and frustration which more than once gifted me a free pass from church. Oh, the delight when I heard the car pulling out of the driveway without me. That trick didn't last long as my parents were good at their own tricks and managed to win at getting me to church.

At thirteen my family moved to Oman in the Middle East for my father's work. As a Muslim country, it was my introduction to a religion other than my own. At first, the daily noise that echoed from the mosques was strange and so unlike the hymns of Sundays back home. Now when I hear the call to prayer I feel comfort, as to me it is the sound of ritual and a marker of the time in my life that I went from girl to teenager: from playing dolls and dress-ups to crushes on boys and my first kiss.

There was a Catholic church in Oman that was more than an hour drive away, in a very hot large hall, filled with Pakistani and Bangladeshi workers who were all converts of the missionaries in their home countries. The heat and the body odor, the bad sound system that warped the already hard-to-understand priest's accent, and the long drive made the trip an even greater discomfort and dread than the Sundays back home. It didn't take long before Saturdays (as the Muslim second day of the weekend) transformed into one of my parents making the trip and the other staying home to watch the clan of Driscoll kids. I did not mind this change in tradition at all. For me, it was easy to let go and to spend my time without a god or a church. I was happy to not be inside a place that always had the effigy of Jesus on the cross that I found no comfort in. I know for many this symbol is a strong affirmation of love and sacrifice but for me, all I see is violence and wish to not look. My everyday knowing of prayer shifted to the call from the mosque and images of prayer rugs and men knelt over and bowing. I noticed this and paid little attention. I learned small parts of the Muslim religion: the Bible had a counterpart in the Quran, and the annual time of reflection and self-sacrifice of Lent at Easter became Ramadan with the day of nothing and the night of everything. Both Lent and Ramadan were practiced by others around me but had almost no influence on my life. As expats, we were segregated and I attended the international school with the many others from countries far away. My interest was on my friends, boys, and the new understanding that we were all from somewhere and the world was a big place.

When I was fifteen we returned to Australia and the call to prayer faded in my memory. My parents made the obvious choice to them and enrolled my sister Sandra and me into the Catholic secondary school in the small town we had moved to. The school itself looked cold and was filled with nuns who in my memory had been mean and unforgiving at primary school – well not all of them, but it is the memory of the mean nun that sticks. My sister and I wanted to go to the public high school that was much bigger, looked way more interesting, and had a cuter uniform. At first, our request was met with a firm no, but persistence does pay off and a deal we could all settle on was struck. For the six months, my father remained in Oman finishing his contract, Sandra and I were to go to church every Sunday without complaint and we were to help and support our mum with the younger ones. We kept up our part of the deal and went to say our amen's and take communion every weekend. Most often we chose the Saturday night mass as it gifted us a sleep-in on Sundays. Six months of Saturday sermons later we stopped going. After all, that was the end of the deal. We were now settled in our new school and mum and dad let it be as they had a lot to do with two new businesses and five children still at home. Maybe they hoped the younger siblings would stay close to God and the church, but alas, all seven of us never did. One by one we left and have now all found our own peace with God, religion, and all that comes with that.

For me, my journey back to spirituality and any talk of Gods was a twisted trail and somewhere in there was teenage angst followed by a curiosity about what else is possible in the realm of miracles. I wanted to play in magic and dreamt of white witches, master healers, and psychic mediums. One of my first tools for learning was the Tarot. How I got my first deck I no longer remember. Maybe I gifted it to myself? I do remember how I loved to learn and read about life lessons and how each card was a step in the bigger journey. Most were learned when I read for others. Young hopefuls would sit opposite me on the floor of our shared living space as they shuffled to see which cards would spell out their fortune. I felt at purpose and powerful with spirit and magic as my allies. At times it felt like I was returning to a far away home. My wish and intention was to be a teacher and a guide. Admittedly, at twenty, this feeling was also mixed with my deep desire to be someone unique. I would work hard to give the wondering and hopeful soul sitting opposite me on our rarely vacuumed, stained Feral Street carpet the best possible version of how to move towards the life they desired. I swam in a world of, "It just may be, just may be wonderful." The world hadn't broken me yet.

I would harbor a small fear that a reading would reveal a horrible or painful next step for my hopeful enquirer. I learnt quickly how to find the silver lining in the cards that held the difficult steps in the journey through the Tarot. So in my telling, death came bearing gifts. Yes, it was an ending but it augurs new beginnings – just as an end of pregnancy gifts you a child. I spent more time talking about the gifts as I was uncomfortable seeing the other through the lens of death. I wished to play with magic, not death. Little did I know that Hades was invisible and sitting with us on the living room floor.

Death has now come to me more than once and I have found that death has been generous. I have received gifts. Admittedly they are hard to unwrap as they are bound in grief. It is in the unwrapping that the grief becomes lighter. In the lightness of the heart, the soul expands.

But what of the moments, weeks, days before death? Do the gifts arrive early to help us prepare for the passing, for the shift that death brings to your soul? And how does one begin to accept a gift from death when death is the very enemy that took your loved one away?

PART ONE
Shadows and Light

The Compass points North.
The needle will always seek North. Our truth.

The Element of Earth.
Rest or the time of darkness. A place of growth,
abundance, death and returning to the earth.
Associated with love spells and fertility.

New Moon.
The time of beginnings and setting an intention.
The darkest hours of the moon.

MY FIRST MEETING WITH GRIEF came through Nick.

"I'm sorry. I love you," he said.

We had been arguing, about us, our future, his life. When he called again I believed he was apologizing for the harsh words flung at each other in our fight earlier.

"I love you too." I instinctively replied.

I had been fighting for us, for him, but he had hit the self destruct button and was at the surrender to the inevitable. I could feel it and had for days and weeks. Nick had struggled for years with his mental health and his deep desire to die. He was actively slipping away. I felt if I held on tight enough, he would have something to hold onto.

Nick and I met at university where we were studying drama and education. In time we became good friends and then, best friends. He was the one I sought company with each day and the man I had fallen in love with. Nick had a mass of dark curls, almond brown eyes and a cheeky grin that begged for tricks and playtime.

To know Nick meant to know of his deep love for Freddie Mercury, lead singer of the band, Queen. Freddie Mercury died in November 1991, the summer before we started university and his loss was felt deeply by Nick. Freddie was not your stereotypical rock star and in him, Nick saw the showman he wished to be. His bedroom walls were covered with posters of Freddie in the throes of performance or posing as the star he was, and every album ever recorded by Queen and Freddie in his solo endeavors were kept as jewels. When he spoke of Freddie he shared stories as though he was his friend and the person in the

13

room who knew him best. It was more than his amazing persona that captured Nick; it was his way of being just left of what others expected and his fantastical way of turning up in the world. The later part of Freddie's life was complicated by AIDS. The disease was a pox on men and the vulnerable. In the eighties and nineties, it was seen as the gay man's disease and the calling card that outed many, and the secret many others kept to themselves and only their trusted circles. There was a rumor of Freddie's sexuality but he never officially came out to declare his supposed love of men. This created a new layer of intrigue and one I think Nick also felt at one with. Like Freddie, Nick was holding a secret. Nick was definitely confused, but I believe it stretched further than young questionings of sexual orientation and more about what type of man he wanted to be.

Nick had created a sense of himself that played in public and another that he knew to be the real him. The public young man was often at tricks, arrogant in his place in the world, and tuned those around him to his liking. The inner world of Nick was tortured and twisted in shame and sorrow that he wore as a cloak of disguise. At first, I was not attracted to him as a kissing potential. I was more interested in what made his grin clip in that way and what he was hiding, as I sensed he held a secret. Looking back now in memory, I imagine I saw his shadow and was in awe of it and how it played out in his life. The details of our unfolding friendship and eventual falling into lovers live now in the midst of memory and reappear as ordinary

14

moments: playing cards on the carpet, scraping together dollars to buy beer or a bud of green pot to smoke, listening to music, sharing time with others. I can still see myself sitting on the front steps at Feral Street waiting to see his yellow car spin around the corner. I know our relationship was at first slow and built a moment at a time with much laughter, silliness, challenge and the exploration of our developing selves. It was in those many ordinary moments that the cloak was pulled away and trust was built.

For three years we played in our world at university as drama students. It truly was a performance with each player doing their best to make their scene shine. We were all playing grown-ups in a show we were happy to star in. Our days existed to be together. Sure we learned some stuff at lectures or tutorials but the true learning was within each other and often found at the Normanby Hotel down the hill from our university. A quick flash of your student card earnt you a $5 jug of cold beer that would be shared with the players as we sat under the large Moreton Bay Fig trees of the beer garden. Under those trees we debated, laughed, fought and tested every theory of life and love known to us. There was a full cast of players, each taking their turn in the spotlight, each taking turns to hurt, delight or challenge the other, just as a good drama demands.

As the script dictated, Nick and I spent time loving and hurting each other – again and again. Always to return to the other in the hope we would be forgiven and allowed to share time and the next scene together. We often allowed each other to fuck up – me more than him, but we both fucked up. He broke my heart more than once and I let him. Few people knew of Nick's morbid thoughts and his detailed plans of death at his own hands, but it was me he would call in the middle of the night to tell me he was close to jumping or indulging in a cocktail of pills. I would make my way to him, to rescue, to remind him of the silver linings of life, and to keep him in earth time.

Nick did make attempts at death and at living. In the last months of our third year at university, he shared his despair with his parents and was given a treatment plan that worked – for a short while.

Prozac wasn't the answer apparently. Instead, we smoked pot in our many handmade bongs, drank beer, and on occasion played in the wonder world of LSD. My fight with him was my attempt to get us clean, to seek the straight and narrow for a while, to find our way through the mental health drug haze we navigated daily.

The energy had been twisting and the tension was getting tighter around his death desire. Nick was in trouble and we both knew it. He had been reckless and time was running out. He spoke of leaving town, for a fresh start. I did not want him to leave but if that kept him alive I was all for the plan. Days before his exit he came to me and asked if there was anything I needed from him – he was willing to give me whatever I wanted and thanked me for being his friend.

"Just you," I said.

That night we slept together for the last time and it felt final. As he slept in my bed I took myself away to the shower to cry in peace. My deep desire was to save him from himself. I wanted to be the woman who made him stay, not to stay with me, but to simply stay. I wished to be the white witch healer who could transform pain into possibility. In truth, we were young kids lost in playing with death and magic and were in way over our heads.

The night he called to say "I love you" was the last time I heard his voice. That night Nick killed himself. His apology was not for his harsh words but for the planned actions that he knew would cause me pain. I felt a strong pull that night. I wanted to run to him. The rain was heavy and constant and kept me from running, as did my feeling that just as Nick was, I needed to let go. It felt like I was a violin being played and the tune had gone on too long. It was time to snap the strings and stop the song. I simply didn't realize that stopping the song meant death.

The next morning our friend Kurt called from a nearby telephone booth. When I picked up the phone I heard distress and simply the words:

"He did it. Nick is dead. He killed himself."

Still in my pajamas, I dropped the phone and ran. Nick lived three streets away across the park and on the main road. I arrived at his house to find Kurt in horror tears and Nick dead in his car, sitting peacefully in the passenger seat, a tape of Pink Floyd's The Wall ejected from the car's cassette player. I remember thinking that odd as we never listened to Pink Floyd together, we had been playing Nick Cave and the Bad Seeds new album and often fell asleep to the tune of our favorite track: The Ship Song.

Slowly the players gathered for our most tragic scene, the death scene we had all missed but were now playing out in our minds. We were all lost in the not knowing of how death was to be played out and what happened next.

That evening, lost in the not knowing, I got on my hands and knees and began scrubbing the filthy bathtub at Feral Street. I remember feeling strange but at purpose. My body was raging with a mix of shaking emotions and disturbing numbness that drove my need to scratch at something. I didn't know yet how to ground myself and the energy pulsing was seeking a foundation. Scrubbing the bath made the most sense to my shocked brain.

Death had arrived and I saw no gifts. My guilt was thick and missing my friend was all-encompassing. We were a month away from the end of the year and summer was upon us but nothing felt bright. Comfort was nowhere and everyone around me was as lost as I was in the unknowing of how to grieve. My energy was restless as I sought a space or place that would ease the rumble of emotion passing through me. My mother came to town to sit with me, yet I could not sit. I chose to run. I had a sense that staying with the discomfort was the task of grief, but my desire to flee was strong and had me crying on a bus as it drove North. Before I left, my mother asked me why I was going, what I was seeking. I had no answer other than I need to. I traveled north to my old school town to see a good friend, Kate, and then further to the top corner of the state to see another friend, Julie. Each arrival gave me a new loved one to hug and a moment of relief that quickly tumbled into the mess of my mind and heart. I craved a place of peace where my grief and guilt did not or could not enter. The bus trips between towns were long and shifted me in location but not in feeling. The discomfort was now my normal, no matter where I was.

It was much later after Nick's death that my sister Heather told me that Dad had cried the day he heard of Nick's suicide. She shared with me how surreal it was to see our father cry. I could only imagine as I had never seen my father's tears. This added to my knowing that the heart and soul had shifted for not just me, but many of us. Death can have that effect.

The months that followed were the extended version of drama school games mixed with the heightened emotions of grief. We were all so young and knew very little about how to truly support each other and how to navigate death. We tried and in truth did the best we could at the time with the little we knew of the world and its lessons. Mostly I felt guilt. I missed my friend and was heavy with the knowing that despite my efforts I did not save him.

My friends Nina and Jess, who I shared a home with, moved us out of our share house on Federal St and further away from the scene of death. In truth it was not further away; it was the place I saw death from a new angle. It was an effort towards a fresh start, perhaps a gift. My bedroom in that house I adorned with many candles that I would light each night to mourn, cry and grate over my guilt. In the dark is where grief lived her full self and the candles aided as protective light as I was afraid not of the dark, but of being swallowed by grief. Not every night, but enough nights to create a pattern, my bed would shake slightly. It felt like the rocking of a cradle. I created a narrative that it was angels who were there to soothe me. Nick's death returned me to a relationship with angels as I had a reason to reach to them now. I came to love the rocking and would miss it on the nights it did not arrive. On odd unexpected nights, my bed rocks now and I feel again the rocking and care of angels and I share a moment in love with Nick.

THE FIRST CHRISTMAS after Nick's death the family gathered in Sydney at my sister Kath's home. It was good to be together as a clan again but my heart was not in celebration. I desired retreat and stillness and had little want for connection or conversation. My elder sister Kath found me one day sitting alone outside and sat with me. In the silence that followed I found words to express the loss and guilt I felt. Kath did her best to comfort me with wise words of the elder sister, but in truth, there was no comfort. Later that day, while resting alone, Kath brought me her copy of a book she recently read that she felt I may enjoy. The book was Mists of Avalon by Marion Zimmer Bradley. It is the story of the time of King Arthur told through the women in his life: his mother, sister, aunt, and wife. The book became my playground as I indulged in the stories of the women and their connection to magic, healing, and the power of Avalon. In them I saw myself in the image I created as the best version of me: the white witch healer. A little piece of magic returned to my world through that book. My favorite character, Morgaine, begins the book with the words:

> *In my time I have been called many things: sister, lover, priestess, wise woman, Queen. Now in truth, I have come to be wise woman and a time may come when these things need to be known. But in sober truth, I think it is the Christians who will tell the last tale. Forever the world of Faery drifts further from the world in which the Christ holds sway.*

I saw through her, a narrative bigger than me, one of the old traditions clashing with the new Christian way and religion, of women being honored and then feared. My horizon of god and magic widened. I spent our time together as a family lost in the narrative and missed the story playing out in front of me.

THE NEW YEAR BEGAN and charged with my refreshed relationship to magic I tried my best at healing and sat by my candles at night and wished upon peace. The truth was I had numbed most of my grief and was foolishly thinking that it would simply melt away like the candle wax that dripped each night. I didn't work at working through, I denied, swallowed and powered on.

At the time I had a youth and education theatre company that I ran with two friends, Hayley and Nadine. We had a new performance we had been devising that would premiere at a high school. Our first show written the year before was a hit, our second was not. We three knew it but also knew we were booked and expected to show up. The day before our booking I was in the city at an appointment furiously learning lines and trying to manage the overwhelming feelings of how unready we were for the performance. On my way home on the bus I played with imagination and magic and asked the universe to bring a reckoning.

"Please, make something happen that prevents this show opening tomorrow. Please!"

I got home to find my sisters, Sandra and Judith, standing in my living room. Their faces were shadowed and looked tortured. My sister Sandra stepped towards me and broke my heart with three words.

"Dad died today."

The show did not go on.

The second death tore me off center and affected not only me but my whole family. We were all now staring at death and waiting for the grief waves to pull us under. My father had suffered a heart attack and was gone before I even knew his heart was tensing under the pressure of staying alive. Everything felt surreal and life twisted to reflect this. The day of my father's funeral a limousine arrived to take us to the chapel. Liz, the youngest of us, aged 9 almost 10 at the time, was excited to see the limousine and even more excited to ride in it. Her excitement transformed into a tornado of tears in the chapel as she sat on my lap and howled as the priest shared prayers and blessings.

After the service the limousine drove my family, in silence and pain, to the cemetery. It felt strange and disquieting to walk out onto the lawn with my mother, sisters, and brother and to be met by a large hole of earth and my father in a box of carved wood.

When he passed I had not seen my father for months as he lived with my mother and two sisters, Heather and Liz (the little ones), in the Solomon Islands, where he was at work transforming their education system. The last time I saw him I remember the hug he gave me before getting into the taxi to the airport. It was a tighter hug than he normally gave and included a heavy repeated pat on the back. I remembered that hug in the days that followed his death. I was thankful I had told him I loved him and knew that he was proud of me.

Colin, my father, was a power force and the leader our family rotated around. He was magnificent, smart, fun and supportive. My parents had a strong marriage and created a clan with seven children and a whole lot of love. I often thought myself lucky to be in a strong and loyal family; at times we felt invincible. My father's death made it clear that even strong families can suffer.

STANDING AT THE OPEN GRAVE with the mourners gathered, we silently listened to the final prayers of the priest. The coffin had been crafted by Solomon Islanders in the days that followed my father's death. It was made of heavy wood and carvings and was sealed and ready to be released into the earth, to be forever gone.

As the coffin is lowered, it jars and halts, sitting half in and half out of the grave. The sun had begun to set and the head of the coffin was propped up in perfect alignment to take in the sunset view. My father loved sunset and would sit in the best vantage position, with a drink in hand, and let the day rest as the sun set. The last sunset for my father and he was unwilling to surrender – the coffin did not fit. The standard size of a coffin in Australia was obviously smaller than a handcrafted coffin made in the Solomon Islands. The scene was bizarre, distressing and uncomfortable. This is when my mother cracked wide open and walked away. I followed her as she left the gravesite and retreated behind a small bushy tree, hidden from all mourners and away from the site of my father's almost-descent to earth. The tension my mother was holding radiated off her in sharp daggers of hurt and pain. In silence we stood hidden and smoked a cigarette. At the grave the gravediggers were at task making the hole larger. I remember musing in my mind that they should have known, not that the coffin would be too big, but that my father was a large man in spirit and personality, and he would resist leaving earth time in any way he could. The last sunset disappeared with my father's coffin under earth and buried in what was now the family plot.

Growing up I spent a lot of time in the shadow of my dad. He felt so strong and powerful that to be close to him meant to step into his shadow. To him, I was the smart one. My elder sisters Sandra and Kathy were the dancers and I was the smart one (and despite my desire to be so, was and still am, an uncoordinated awkward dancer). My dad, an academic with a ferocious appetite for learning, would indulge me in discovery. We studied the map of the world and together memorized the capital of all 50 states of the USA so we could test each other. At night, after he arrived home from work, I would sit with him while he watched the news so I was in prime position to share our favorite show that followed: Inspector Gadget. When our family purchased our first at home computer I was the child given the most time at the screen. The reasoning behind this was because I was the smart one. My father had seven degrees, two of them doctorates. Intelligence meant everything to my father and he saw that in me. One of his favorite questions was; "What do you want to be when you grow up?"

I learned years later that as a child I was free with my connection to spirit. I vibed with a different tune of intelligence. I spoke openly about what I saw as to me it was natural. Growing up in a Catholic family this was not normal or wanted. The fear was that I would be damned or shunned. I remember none of this, I know only through hypnosis. In my thirties, I worked as a massage therapist and Reiki practitioner in a clinic with other healers and practitioners. My friend Krissy was learning hypnosis and I gladly accepted the invitation to be her guinea pig. I was most interested in my own healing and my scarce memories of my intuitive abilities as a child, so we started there. While under hypnosis I saw myself as a young girl of four, sitting on my bed crying, telling my spirit friends that they needed to go and leave me as they were not allowed. How I knew or felt this, I do not know. When I tried to reach further into the memory under hypnosis I saw only black. I was told through spirit I was being protected by my parents. To them, my seeing was dangerous, not that they had ever told me that, but it was what I felt. I wanted to please them and be a good girl so I told my spirit friends to leave. My seeing stopped and my intelligence became centered upon what logic and intellect allowed. I have never felt anger or anguish about this early memory. I have always known my parents wanted the best for me and did everything in their power to make it so. I have forever been and continue to be someone who acknowledges that as far as families go, I got a good one. I wished to be the perfect blend of my parents; intelligent, driven and generous like my father and nurturing, caring and creative like my mother. I felt assured that when I grew up I would have lots of children and a loving husband. I wanted to recreate the family I had been born into.

TWO SHIFTS OF THE SOUL seven months apart. Death was now normal and grief was ever-present.

I was twenty-one.

One day shortly after my father passed the pressure built in my chest and I felt my own heart tensing. I was very much alive but not sure if I wanted to be. I wandered around my home lost with a heaviness that was growing. I went into the bathroom to wash my face, to get a grip. My knees buckled and I found myself on the floor of the bathroom sobbing, holding my knees, crouched under the sink. It was not my father I was crying for. Or for Nick. It was for me.

"I can't do this again," I repeated over and over and felt the intense guilt of selfishness.

I had no idea how I was going to get up off the floor, let alone move forward. Grief sat heavy as a weight on my heart. Grief was in no way melting away. She had come to stay.

As I had done months before, I worked hard at powering on and not at working through. It became easier to ignore the pain as there was a steady supply of beer and marijuana that assisted in the numbing of it all. My mother was coping as best she could. She moved back to Australia and set up a home. It was good to have us all together but there was the very real missing of our father and for my mother her soul mate.

Weeks after my father's death my mother's father died in the United States. Like me, my mother had lost two men whom she loved dearly so close together in time. Grief sat with her twice over and silenced connection to others. My mum is not a woman of many words and as a family, we followed her lead and didn't speak much of death or our feelings. Driscolls have a tendency to power on, and on most days it proves to be a strength. On the days that bring death, not so much.

Time ticked over and the anniversaries came and went. The first year without my father at Christmas, the first anniversary of Nick's passing, the first year my birthday was without either of them. My knowledge of grief at the time was that it takes about a year, so I had been told, somewhere, somehow. I moved forward with an assurance that the new normal was coming and I would eventually feel okay. My feelings were not felt, they were numbed, and the pressure in my head and heart built. I knew I was not okay but did very little to help myself so the tension continued to gain strength until it broke. I again found myself in a bathroom, this time in a different share house, sitting down in the shower one morning, holding my knees and crying without end. My squashed grief had won and had left me without the will or energy to stand. The idea of finishing my shower and starting my day was too much to bear. It was that morning in the shower, almost two years after Nick's death and beyond the first anniversary of my father's passing that I first surrendered.

Grief begged my attention and I gave it to her. In order to cope I was prescribed antidepressants and referred to a psychologist. I hated the idea of taking the pills, after all, I was the girl who could always find the silver lining, so I made a promise to myself. I promised I would sit with grief and find my way back to steady ground. I vowed to swallow the pills and see the psychologist every week until I could get through the day without crying or denying.

When grief came crashing in, I did not recognize her. I did not connect that my feelings and sad reality were the culmination of missed moments of grief. I was still of the belief that the time had passed, it was more than a year, and by now it surely must be something else. I had no other way of knowing grief, and no rituals, community space or shared language to invite her in. All I had was the idea of a year of mourning and something about 5 stages that I didn't pay much attention to. This is when I learned that grief is patient and persistent and will wait to be attended to. There is no sidestepping her. She will continue to tap your heart until she is acknowledged and felt. I promised myself that if grief ever came to meet me again, I would not deny her.

My healing journey beyond weekly appointments with the psychologist and daily medication opened a doorway to the healing arts that are not of doctors or man-made medicine. My first exploration was in aromatherapy and the power of oils as magic. I enrolled in evening classes and each week I felt a growing sense of coming home again. As my learning progressed I began to blend and create magic potions for myself and eventually for others who were interested in the potential of magic and in their own way were seeking a healing balm. I read of fairies and their ways, of angels and their blessings, and began to weave a world that felt in tune with me.

Grief slowed down to an almost silent pulse only getting louder at anniversaries and birthdays and on an odd day that grief simply had something to say. I missed my father but had learned to live in a world without him, and Nick I imagined had moved on to new dramas in the universe and I wished him well.

MY WORLD WIDENED and I set forth traveling with my friend, now partner, Nina. We backpacked through Europe on a quest to see what the rest of the world looked and felt like. Nina and I were seeking the possibility of living overseas and creating a life together. We found adventures but not a way forward. It was love that brought me home six months later. Jess, our Feral St partner in crime and good friend was marrying her sweetheart David and I was one of her bridesmaids. I came home to honor their love and union and broke my own. I never returned to Europe or to Nina. It was hard to not fly back but I felt propelled by a forward movement and the crafting of new beginnings. I moved south to Melbourne to deepen my new world.

I was twenty-five.

On my journey south with the new bride, Jess, my backpack – loaded up with the pieces that would lay the foundation of my new life – was stolen out of her car while we blissed out on a beach having lunch and a swim. I arrived in Melbourne with a small box of pictures and other treasures, my handbag, and the clothes on my back. I had lost Nina, our future, and now all of my belongings that connected to that past. A new start was now a material and emotional reality. The thief ignited both anger and relief in me. I was angry that my world as I had packed it was stolen. Relief came later as I felt the lack of baggage that I carried into my new city. A clean slate of possibilities lay before me.

In Melbourne, I knew two people: Julie, a good friend from high school and Kurt, one of the players at the time of the first death. I quickly went from lost to found and connected to the people and places they introduced me to. I moved into an apartment above a chicken shop in the soon-to-be very trendy North Fitzroy with Kurt and his friend Josh, a musician. Life was good, I was beginning again and everything felt fresh, a blessed relief from my broken heart woes felt after separating from Nina.

An almost immediate connection was made with Chris, a lad about my age and a good friend of Josh. Chris was my mirror image. I had just returned from Europe and he was soon to be on his way across the pond to London. Connecting with him felt easy and time-limited as he was set to fly in a matter of weeks. We spent time with the gang going to live music events in Fitzroy, a short tram ride or longer walk away. We enjoyed dancing, laughter, beer, lots of beer, and the stolen moments alone. We connected more deeply than I think either of us expected and we both played at games of staying cool and being easy. I was excited to connect to another but aware that I had not given space for my relationship of years with Nina to breathe and recover from severance. The beer and music helped to let it all flow forward. After all, Chris would soon be gone and the next chapter would begin, so I told myself.

It was a surprise to us both when I found the two pink lines on the stick that spelled pregnancy. Two pink lines and two weeks of Chris left in the country. My decision was not immediate. In conversation with Chris, who said he would support whatever decision I made, I knew it was all too fast and not in the best interest of me or Chris. I released and let go. The pregnancy was terminated and Chris left. A different version of death had arrived to meet me and despite my promise, I denied grief. I washed my face, put on some lipstick and powered on. I got a new job as a youth worker and explored study in natural remedies. I tried to study herbalism and failed, dropping out in the third week. I convinced my mother to pay for a course in Traditional Chinese Massage, I went each week, barely taking in the learning and scraping through on my last exam.

Nine months after the pregnancy I came home to find Julie in our kitchen of the home we shared in a new house around the corner from the chicken shop.

"Jules, so strange, all day my lower back and belly have been aching. Aching in a way they never do."

Julie, being a long time silent seer, gently gazed at me and said nothing for a short while.

"I was wondering if you would feel anything," she said.

"Feel what?" I responded just in time before sensation hit and in a flash, I added the days and weeks to realize it was nine months later and my body was feeling the baby that was not to be. A stabbing pain ran through my lower torso and I fell into tears and released a sob from my soul. Grief had found me at the not-to-be birth of my first child.

Grief and Julie sat with me as loss washed over and away. I lay for only a short time, maybe two days. My knowing habit was to feel, feel deeply and quickly, and then rebuild upon it. To me, it felt like I was moving on but in truth it was an act of burial, to cover over with the earth. In my soul I visited several burial sites that still called me, in my earth reality they were not sacred sites, they were times that had passed and lessons to be absorbed. Each time I denied grief my soul thinned just a little, not enough to notice in the moment, but enough to create vulnerability. As I sought joy it escaped me, just a beat away. I surmised a state of not learning enough, that I was to try harder at getting it, to powering on and reaching further.

Denial of grief equals lack of joy, two sides of the same coin. Our soul naturally seeks the full expression of both, but joy is allowed and grief is something to be shared at a funeral, on an anniversary, or in private moments that will not disturb others not open or able to witness her. Again, grief sat with me and I did not recognize her. My sadness was covered over with everyday life and the eroding of self-love. My journal entries spilled stories of feeling not good enough, unloveable, and the one that would never get the happily ever after story that others seemed to be achieving.

The Christmas of 2000 I chose to stay in Melbourne and not travel north to be with my family. Others around me had places to be, celebrations to attend, and gifts to open. I was alone and felt it. I had spent very little time alone as I was one of seven, who had beyond my family created homes with friends. I had a life filled with others and being alone was scary as in the silence I heard echoes of my pain. Loneliness and Christmas are good friends and often buddy up to sit with and bully bruised or grieving hearts.

Over the horror of enduring the holiday season, I had slipped further into my sadness. Grief sat with me in the stillness and I chose not to look at her. While reluctantly driving to a Christmas party, I found myself turning to peer into the back seat of my car, this was repeated at each red light. In my imagining there was a baby seat with a baby of my own strapped in and smiling at me. As a young girl I dreamt of being a mother – at twenty-seven my biological clock began to tick and loneliness turned up the volume. Tick, tock, tick-tock. Bah Humbug!

On New Year's Day of 2001, I was sitting in a slumped position in my living room nursing the mandatory New Years day hangover with my good friend Josh.

"So what's your wish? What do you want this year?" He asked.

Without a thought I replied

"I want to have a baby."

"What! Really?"

I was shocked to hear the words flow out so easily and I began to cry. Josh moved closer to me and asked softly.

"Is that what you really want?"

I wasn't so sure but my sense was the answer was yes.

By August it was cold and my desire for a child was not completely forgotten but had slid back into the odd daydream. The reality of a child and my own family seemed far away as I had been repeating my pattern of almost-love with a variety of not quite-right-men and my track record did not make me a bookie's safe bet. I spent time drifting to a future me that had achieved the sought after happily ever after and I was thin, fabulous, loved, and surrounded by children and a husband that loved me. Deeper into the image, I'm wearing a white gown that flows and graces my curves, my hair is perfect and every scar on my body is gone. I was the white witch mother, lover, and healer and had never looked or felt better. The more I imagined the mythical future me, the worse I felt about the lumpy awkward self that was smiling on the outside desperate to cover over my fear of being exposed as ordinary and fractured.

One night in August I found myself at a local bar I knew well, on my own, sitting with my thoughts and a pint of beer. I had returned a day early from a trip away and nobody knew I was back. I wanted it that way so I could steal one more night with my thoughts. I sat content on my own, a state I was becoming accustomed to and had begun to seek.

As I drank my beer I reached for my cigarettes and realized I didn't have a lighter. I swept the bar with my eyes and saw an animated and odd-looking middle-aged woman close by, chatting away and smoking. I moved toward her with a cigarette in hand.

"Can I have a light?" I asked.

"Can I have a cigarette?" she replied.

A strange request I thought seeing as she was the one smoking. We shimmered through the crowd to my corner position and exchanged a cigarette for a light and she pocketed the extra cigarette I gave her.

"What is your name?" she asked.

"Debra."

"Debra, you should meet my friend Shaun." she encouraged. I never did get her name.

"Oh no, I'm ok. Happy to be on my own."

And with a side glance and a grin, she blended back into the crowd.

My thirst ordered a second beer and I swore two beers was it and I would make my way home. Halfway through my second beer, habit had me reaching for a cigarette. Knowing how it would play out, I sought the animated women, with a cigarette for her already in hand. Dressed in color with fabrics adorning her hair, she was easy to spot in the crowded bar.

"Hello again. A cigarette for you. May I have a light?"

"Oh good, you are here. This is my friend, Shaun"

Standing beside her was a man not much taller than me with dark shaggy hair that sat just above his shoulders. I locked eyes with him and we did the obvious thing and said hi. A lit cigarette later I returned to my half-drunk pint.

As I was draining the last of my you-promised-yourself-only-two-beers-then-home beer, Shaun found his way to me in my corner.

"Can I buy you a beer?"

I hesitated. Two beers I had promised myself. My moment of hesitation lingered and then landed. What could one more beer hurt?

After the standard polite awkward conversation I said to him;

"Your friend is very interesting."

"What friend?"

"Her," I said as I gazed over the crowd looking for her. The woman with the lighter was nowhere to be seen.

"The woman who introduced us," I said.

"She is not my friend, I don't know her."

"But she said to me, you must meet my friend Shaun."

"Ah, that's strange. She said to me, you must meet my friend Debra. I thought you knew her."

We sat in the moment of friendly trickery, wondering about who she was and just as questions may have been raised a new beer was ordered and the evening shifted to many drinks, singing, and drunken conversation heard over a crowded bar that was warm inside against the bitter winter outside. Shaun was my kind of attractive with a disheveled look of naughty in his grin and an accent from far away. I was happy to play along for an evening of 'maybe never see you again' fun. Why would you not stay? Stay we did until the last call. By then we were beyond drunk and followed the obvious narrative of the naked ending.

I felt lost the next morning after he left. I sat, hungover in the back courtyard of the home I shared with my friend Justine. I was confused as I could not place the feeling that pulsed through my vulnerability. Justine came to join me for morning coffee and last night's gossip. "You're home early. Home to see someone perhaps? I heard a man's voice last night." That was my cue to begin the blow by blow recall of the night's adventures. Instead, I found myself sharing more about my confusing feelings of the morning. As Justine prodded further into my thoughts trying to understand it fell out of me.

"I can't do this again," I said

"Do what?" Justine asked

"I don't know. I just know that this feels strange. Maybe it's time to change or something. I don't know, but something feels not right."

My pulse found a memory lost from long ago and a sense of connection came over me. And a sense of betrayal. I was not sure if I would ever see Shaun again but knew at that moment that I had met him before – just not in this life. My knowing of past lives was almost non-existent at the time and the strong memory shuddered my soul and left me feeling raw. How could I know that about him, and why did his presence feel so strong and a danger to me?

Days later I was out with friends again in the standard rhythm of beer, dancing and twenty-something behavior. I got home late to find Justine still up.

"Shaun came to see you tonight. He stayed for hours. He sat on the couch waiting for you."

"What did he want?"

"He just said he needed to see you. He didn't say much. He played with the dog and waited. He only just left."

Now I was even more confused and my past hurtful feelings disappeared as intrigue entered. What did he want?

A few nights later there was a knock at my door. Shaun stood at the threshold and I let him in. Almost immediately he launched in with questions.

"I have a strong feeling that won't go away. It feels like you have something of mine. Is there something you have to tell me." he said.

"No, I have nothing. It is you who has something for me."

41

He shared with me the feeling he had after our drunken slam into each other. They were his feelings but so uncannily similar to mine. In sober stunned silence, we fell into each other again never finding what it is we shared or the source of our questions.

Over the next few weeks we fell again and again into each other, always with a knock at my door and me opening to let him in. Once he sought to be with me outside of my bedroom.

"Maybe we could go and grab some breakfast together?" he enquired one morning as we woke.

"Yeah sorry, I have meetings at work this morning." I didn't have any meetings booked. What I did have was a knowing that I could invite this man into my bed but not my world.

The feeling of betrayal from the past sat in convenient denial until one night. The way he was, the way it made me feel, the sense memory was so strong. I got out of bed, got dressed and asked him to leave. He was angry at the turn of events and my pushing away to the point that he pushed me by the shoulder down the hallway. I did not fall, I stumbled. Rather than be shaken, I was resolved. It was over and Shaun needed to leave. Now.

I felt the mark of Shaun for the weeks that followed but spoke little of it and instead drank and partied by night and focused on my work by day. My career, as a youth worker and community artist, was finally making tracks into something sustainable and I leaned on the fact that, if nothing else, I could get the career part of my life working.

I had recently finished a youth circus project that was a great success and was on the way to signing a three-year city council contract to build a youth circus and theatre troupe in an inner-city Melbourne suburb. A three-year contract was liquid gold to a freelance artist and I held onto the possibility as my lifeline.

One night I found myself drinking wine with my friend Stephanie, who had lived with Julie and I in the house around the corner from the chicken shop, but now lived with another friend of ours, Robbie. We both mulled over our broken love lives. She had for years been in an intense bond with Josh that had broken, and I was the girl forever without a boyfriend. I had fallen into Shaun and she had fallen into another, for comfort, we told ourselves.

Reaching for my wine glass I moaned about my late period, my crazed and heightened pre-period emotions and how sore my swollen breasts were. As my hand touched the glass my heart skipped a beat and the possibility that I could be pregnant flashed into sight. I said nothing and took a big gulp of the wine. In my early encounters with Shaun we had not been safe and I feared a seed had been planted. I promptly sought the morning after pill and felt like I had dodged a bullet. Being pregnant to Shaun was not my happily ever after wish. As the pill shifts the cycle of the blood, I was lost in counting days and it was very possible the slip of a moment had planted the seed I feared, yet so desired.

Days later I drove to the meeting that heralded my career success. I happily signed on the dotted line and secured the sought after three-year arts contract. Driving away from that meeting it became clear what I needed to do. I pulled into a pharmacy and purchased the pregnancy test I did not want to take but knew I had to.

The positive result was not a shock but it did shake me to the point of losing my grip and falling to the floor. Lost in the moment I didn't hear Justine come home for lunch. She found me gripping a door frame in an effort to stand with a river of tears pouring down my face.

"Whoa. What's up? Are you ok?"

"Juzz, I'm pregnant,"

"Oh fuck, really?"

We sat in silence. Justine is my friend who tells it like it is and is one of the most grounded, non-bullshit women I know, so no words of cliche or hollow thoughts were shared.

"Do you know what you want to do?" she asked.

"I'm keeping the baby."

"Really. Maybe you should think about it for a bit."

For me, there was no choice. I knew my heart would not survive another termination and I felt fate had come to meet me. It was in no way the fantasy I wished for, but my baby had come.

An hour later Justine left for work and I did what I knew I needed to. I called my friends Julie and Mardi to tell them the news. They both promised to get to me as soon as possible and we all made plans to meet in the courtyard at my house. In the time between Justine leaving and waiting for Mardi and Julie to arrive I began to swim in my thoughts and drown in my feelings. I counted the days and recalled the days after blood and my times with Shaun. I thought I was being safe but obviously not as the seed inside me told a different story. In the past weeks I had enjoyed more than a few parties and had indulged in a cocktail of twenty-something delights that promise to bring joy but in truth were covering up the lack of it. One recent Saturday night with Mardi, in the kitchen I shared with Justine, we were again indulging and knowing that we had been doing so for weeks in a row.

"Something needs to change Mardi. It feels like there is no stop button but I need to stop. Maybe I need something to come to force the change."

I thought back to that moment and realized the change had already come and was in my belly waiting for me to tune in. I had no knowledge of pregnancy and what was or had happened to the baby seed as I numbed and denied my nights away. I added up the different events and was struck by a thought. What could one more night hurt? Surely if the damage had been done it was done already. It is amusing how the brain can spin the narrative one wants to hear. Convinced that no more harm could be done I drove to my denial. Wine and cigarettes were purchased and taken to the courtyard to await my friends. I didn't wait, I poured myself a glass of red wine, lit a cigarette, and ceremoniously cheered the air and announced to the universe that Debra was having a baby. I can't remember who arrived first, but I do remember that both Julie and Mardi had the same response to the glass of wine in one hand and the cigarette in the other. They both gently enquired if I was ok and if this meant denial of the baby seed.

"I'm keeping the baby and we are celebrating as tonight is my last chance to drink for a long time and right now I need to drink."

"So, let's drink." my friends responded.

A few hours later Justine came home to find the party in the courtyard and did the same with inquiry and then surrender to the wine. As the wine loosened my thoughts the sensations of what was before me began to fill in and create the image of a very different future than my imagination had previously crafted. It scared the shit out of me while simultaneously bringing me a feeling of possible joy and delight. My hangover the next morning was severe and steeped in guilt.

I let nights pass so I could sort through my feelings. My feelings or thoughts did not change: I was keeping the baby. I was scared but ready. As I knew Shaun mostly naked I had no idea about how he would react when I shared the news. I knew he spent a lot of time at the pub I met him in so I searched for him there. I was nervous but resolved as I swung open the door.

"Ah! It is my friend Debra!"

The animated and odd women who I had not seen since the night I met Shaun was seated at the bar close to the door and announced my entrance. The lads by the pool table all looked up, including Shaun. Feeling vulnerable and exposed, I shifted towards the woman in a defensive move.

"Tell me, how are you and my friend Shaun getting along?"

"Oh, I'm not sure actually. I am here to figure that out."

"Well, I hope you can be friends."

I wasn't sure what I hoped for but I was about to find out.

Stranger than seeing her again was the child seated on her lap. The child must have been two or three years old and was silently sitting folded into the woman's chest. As I look back on her and retell the story she became known as the Gypsy woman with the child. I am not sure if she was an earth angel or the mystery of magic playing tricks on me. The only thing I am sure of is, she had a mission to ensure Shaun and me met. I never saw her or the child again.

Shaun was surprised to see me and I got the sense he saw me as the woman who felt she had made a mistake and wanted him back and in my bed. I invited him to a table in a dark secluded corner so we could talk.

"Shaun, I'm pregnant," was met by "I am not ready to be a father," followed by pressure to terminate. He wanted "it" gone and his words cut as if he was scraping away the child in the hope we could imagine "it" had never happened. No responsibility for his part to play ever entered the heated and hurtful conversation. We circled around each other never coming to the center and not allowing the truth of the other to penetrate or shift our standing. I shared about my past pregnancy and how my heart would not withstand another termination; he shared his poor relationship with his own father and his unwillingness to be close to any father, his own or the potential one inside him. We shared stories but did not listen to the other. The betrayal was ever-present and no longer a sense memory but my reality. We rose to a crescendo.

"Shaun, do you want me to just walk away?"

"Yes."

I rose at purpose with my heart frozen solid and shattering all at once. I walked away with the sense of betrayal intact – again.

The days that followed were a haze of hurt, anger and the deepening sense of betrayal. The unyielding part was the shame and anger I turned onto myself. I had been a willing participant in the story and was now the one literally left holding the baby. The shame was the most distressing as it emerged from deep inside my long-forgotten Catholic veins. I was to have a bastard child. An unwed scarlet woman I had become, and the heavy weight of guilt that is the forever-friend of Catholics settled over me like a second skin. I was awed by the power of prayer and felt the presence and fear of sin settle deep inside. I don't remember listening or caring as I sat through the mornings in church as a young girl, but Catholic guilt was ever-present and was burning as it ran through me.

Alone one night in my room I allowed the guilt and shame to win. I was so unsure if my resolve to keep the baby was right, and if I even deserved it. On my knees, in tears, I implored heaven, Mother Mary, her son, God and all the angels I had assured myself were watching.

"Take my baby if this is your plan for me. If my sin is to

be punished and my shame cut into me then take the baby. I will release and let the baby go if this is your will."

Broken I fell into bed and slept without dreams.

I waited out the days and expected to see the blood that led to death, but it never came. I was not sure if I was relieved. On the third day, I sensed and understood that I was to hold this baby in earth time and my pleading with heaven had given me what I had asked for – someone to love.

PART TWO
In the company of a Sage

The Compass points East.
Where the sun (son) rises. The place of new beginnings
and many lessons.

The Element of Air.
Communication. The power of the mind. New life.

Waxing Moon.
Energy grows and dreams come into the light. The magic
that draws things to you.

Reading a book of spiritual wisdom is not like reading a book of history or political analysis: you are not simply absorbing information – you are spending time in the company of a Sage.

WHILE PREGNANT I WROTE A DIARY to my unborn child. Each day I would share the early stories of life from inside my belly. The idea was gifted to me by my wise mother who after having seven children of her own, knew that the many moments of pregnancy and the early days of a child, while treasured, can be lost, as many memories a child brings. She also thought the writing would help to ease the anger and fear that highlighted the days my son grew inside. One day I wrote and shared with my child that I was unsure of what name to give him and asked him to send me a name. A day and a half later while sitting on the couch tying my shoes, ready to go, I received his name.

"My name is Sage." I heard clearly.

From that moment on, Sage was Sage. Even from the belly Sage was clear, gently directing. The silent teacher.

Sage, my first and only son, the little old man, my master teacher, and a shapeshifter of my world. Sage was the yin to my yang. It took a while to get there but we found balance within our opposites and I felt it deep in my heart when Sage would call me his best friend. I knew in time and maybe so did Sage that this was not our first life together. Over time we have continued to find each other. In this life, I was lucky enough to be his mum.

On the 3rd of May, 2002 I arrived at the hospital flanked by my 'mother to be' support team: Mardi and Julie. By mid-morning, my pregnancy was induced. The day of the 3rd we waited, played cards and told stories, but no change or contractions came. On the day of the 4th, my waters were broken by a kind young doctor who assured me it was all going to be okay.

The day of the 4th was a long, hard day. My contractions developed slowly and the pain steadily increased. By the afternoon, the contractions were enough to inspire groans and whimpers and, to my surprise, visions. As each contraction eased, I was able to decipher what I was seeing, and slowly three images emerged. They were of a woman scared in a dark room laboring alone, a woman on a cot in a big and busy tent laboring among the chaos of an army medical unit, and a woman alone in a bed, legs spread, in tears with blood soaking the sheets. I had no idea who these women were but they were obviously with me as they continued to strengthen and shift with each contraction.

In the early morning of the 5th, I lay with my feet in stirrups surrounded by a midwife, nurses and a doctor, whose hands were deep inside me reaching into my womb. I was crazy tired and had been pushing for hours. My son's first move was to show me his stubborn nature – he gets that from me – by slipping back up the birth canal after each contraction rather than making his way out.

"Ok Debra, we have three more pushes. As you contract I am going to reach in to pull your son out." said the doctor gloved up and looking up at me from between my spread legs.

First push no success and a lot of discomfort and pain. The pain medication they had been dripping into me was ceased earlier so I could feel each contraction and be inspired to push. Inspiration did not come and nor did my son.

Second push. No baby.

"Ok push, push hard. If we don't get this baby out in the next contraction we will have to go to an emergency caesarean."

Third push. No baby.

The doctor, with her hands now out of me, shifted quickly and began barking orders to the nurses, directing me towards the operating table.

"I'm sorry Debra, we need to take you to the operating theatre now. Your baby will be here soon. Don't be disappointed, this is the best way. If this were a 100 years ago you and your baby would have likely died."

The doctor's strange offer of condolence brought back into focus the three women who in vision had shared labor with me.

In a drugged haze, under strong lights in a cold operating room, I surrender to the drugs and the scalpel, and Sage Joseph Driscoll is born screaming on the 5th May 2002.

THE NIGHT SAGE AND I ARRIVED HOME from the hospital all was quiet and still. Sage slept in his cradle in the living room and I lay on the couch. I felt peace flow within me and great responsibility flow toward me. It had been a long while since peace was anywhere in my sphere and I welcomed both peace and Sage home. Sage had safely arrived and now my life was centered on loving him and watching him grow. The responsibility of life as a single mother felt all-encompassing but with the returned peace I felt in Sage's presence it was a task I felt I could do. I knew I could love him as I was already deep in love.

As Driscoll's do, I powered on and took only six weeks off my circus gig to get into the swing of motherhood. I had worked at getting that gig and was confident in telling myself that I could continue as I was before, just now with a babe on my hip or drinking from a boob. As a circus manager, it was the one job a city gal could have that invited and welcomed you to bring your children to work. I was also lucky my city council boss was working towards falling pregnant herself and was very interested and sympathetic to my new life as a mother, as was Sam, my creative partner, and the circus trainer I employed on the gig. He was a part-time parent sharing the care of his young son who would sometimes join us for afternoon training and rehearsal sessions.

Not long after Sage arrived, Chris returned to Melbourne. It felt like some cruel joke that he arrived in mere moments after Sage's birth. Shaun was missing from sight and I had no idea where he was. While pregnant, I thought of him often and wondered what I would do if he returned to my life. For my son I wanted him to return, and for me, I was unsure of what to feel. I was thankful that my heart had never opened to him so his hurt and betrayal could only reach so deep. I ensured he knew how to find us, had told him of Sage's birth but received no response other than silence. Happily ever after was not present. I was alone, but I was in love.

Any mother will tell you that life after birth is never what you imagined, and they are all right! Life as you know it is gone and the demands of your child are your waking pulse. I powered on and felt the essence of me eroding. Sage was literally sucking me dry (he was a hungry kid) and I was still working on being someone and achieving at this thing called life.

One night, while rocking Sage in his cradle begging him to slip into slumber, I heard a voice not my own. It said; "Go North to Queensland." Go North was chanted as I rocked the cradle in the dark. It felt like a call I could not ignore.

The next day I spoke to my mother and shared of the voice in the night that advised me to move to her. As my mother does, she did not tell me what to do, but said;

"You know you and Sage are welcome here."

"Yeah but mum, if I come north I want the full grandma treatment. The help, motherly advice, all of it."

She giggled, just a little. "Of course."

I stayed in Melbourne long enough to direct and showcase the first year's circus performance, a show called Pandolene which translates to Big Sleep. On opening night

Sam came to me very excited with his cheeky well-worn grin.

"I have an idea."

"What now Sam?" I said with my own grin and silliness that we shared, and that had kept us above water as we both navigated life as creative beings and parents.

"Did you know that a baby's hips naturally lock when you hold them by the feet and they stand in perfect alignment? It looks magical – a trick only a babe can do!"

"No, I didn't but I have a feeling I am not going to like what you say next."

"Sage and I can be the opening act!"

"What! You want to hold my twelve-week old baby by the feet on stage."

"Yes! It would be so great."

"Uh, NO!"

"Come on Deb, you know I would never put Sage in any danger."

I hesitated, which spurred on Sam to plead further; "And he has been at every rehearsal, he is a member of our family and he deserves to be in the show."

Sage had been at every rehearsal tied to my chest in a red baby sarong that was his own happy hammock. If ever he grizzled I would slip to the side and shift him in his hammock to meet a boob full of milk that always calmed him. Sam, without pause, would take over the direction and the circus family tumbled on across mats.

Sage held high in the hands of Sam was our opening and closing act of Melbourne. Sage was now literally center stage and in focus. I had weeks before committed to finishing with the troupe and their first performance and then following the voice north. I left days after we closed the show and Sam carried on with the contract and the troupe. I was happy to pass the baton to him and was also happy to finally surrender to motherhood and to Sage. It is easier to see the stones in the path when looking back. I now see the push from the universe to place me where was best was in truth a step back to magic, possibility, and learning the wonders of the world. My world grew as Sage grew.

Surrender is not easy for me. I am a stubborn impatient lass who wants it all now, not always getting it, but working hard to the tune of my stamping feet. My saving graces when I arrived north in Brisbane were my mother and my friend Justine. A few months after my decision to keep Sage, Justine found herself pregnant. As she had, I asked her what she wanted to do and began the lines of …. Of course, any choice you make is okay. In true Juzz style, she cut me short and said, "Yeah but I'm going to keep it." Justine surrendered earlier than me and moved herself and her partner Peter north to Brisbane to be with her family before her son Daniel was born.

Days with a baby melt together. While Sage happily played and discovered the world unfolding before him, I continued my dream of the Disney final scene of the rescued woman who lives the happy ever after story. Damn those fucking fairy tales. Simmering anger at Shaun, and at myself, lay just under the surface. On the surface was the Driscoll determination to not only survive, but to do better, to be the best version of a family I could muster, and to pretend to the outside world that all was fine. My mind fantasized about running away, hiding, moving anywhere that promised a future, moving away from the pain of being alone with a soul to care for that would one day ask me where his father is. The fear had me trapped and it felt like I was treading water.

ALWAYS CHASING AN ADVENTURE or the glimpse of a life worth retelling, one weekend I bundled up nine-month-old Sage and took him out into the forest to meet my friends Justine, Peter and their babe Daniel. Camping with the kids was one of our favorite things to do and really our best option as we were all under the reality of the cash-poor life of raising babes. The sky was thick with clouds and the forecast was not hopeful for a sunny shift, but I was. I drove the hours up the highway and then an hour or so into the forest to meet my friends who had left earlier to set up camp. I arrived just before the rain. Under cover for the night, we drank wine, held our babes, and eventually succumbed to the wet evening and retired. My cheap two-person tent was not a match for the persistent and heavy rain. In the middle of the night I woke to raindrops on my face. Sage, being so small, was still able to easily nestle into my chest, which by the early hours before dawn was the last place inside the tent that was dry. As day broke we gathered under shelter with other campers and studied the sky. To arrive at the site, which was deep into the forest, you crossed over three river fords. The rivers, normally a trickle, and crossed easily without a bridge, were quickly becoming flowing currents of rainwater. My mind scanned the exit through the forest and saw that I was soon to be trapped. It was clear, if Sage and I were to get out I would need to leave soon. I only had enough nappies and babe supplies for another day or so, all our bedding and most of our clothes were wet, and word from the campers was the rain was staying and would if anything, get heavier. My fear of leaving the forest was smaller than my fear that if I stayed Sage would get sick. I made the call and together with Peter, while Juzz watched the babes, packed up my wet gear, crammed it into my small hatchback, and with a quick wave peeled out of the site and into the forest. Justine's face as I drove away mirrored what I felt: fear and the great expanse of the unknown.

I drove carefully and watched through swishing wipers the rain that was not easing. As we arrived at the first river ford, I paused. The water was flowing and I could not tell how deep it was. I had committed to leaving and the only way out of the forest was over the water so I put my foot tentatively on the accelerator and eased in. The car stopped. I was now in the middle of the crossing, stuck in stillness, with Sage strapped in the back peacefully sitting in his chair. He had no idea of the danger and I tried to remain calm so he would not sense my fear. I wait, pray, and then turn the key. The car starts and we move forward out of the water and back onto the mud path that was only yesterday a dirt road. Traveling further I notice there are no other cars or movement, even the birds have retreated to safety.

As I arrive at the second river ford my heart drops and my fear increases. It is obviously deeper. I wait and think, and my only thought is I have to keep moving forward. We are deep into the forest now and I have seen no-one. We are alone and our best chance is to keep moving and get out. I turn to look at Sage. He looks at me and smiles. My sense of responsibility for him is larger than the sanctuary cell inside my small car and I feel like I may suffocate. My foot reaches the pedal and the car pushes forward into the water. To my despair and surprise, the water is deeper than I had thought. The car stops and again we are in the middle of the ford with water lapping up the sides of the car. I begin to pray. After a short time, I try the key. No sound, no movement. I beg angels to get Sage and I safely out of the forest. I look back to Sage and sense the great responsibility of being the only one here and feel the lack of knowing what to do other than pray.

I try the key. No sound, no movement.

My breath is shallow in comparison to the rising depth of the water. Close to tears looking back to my smiling babe, I pray again, this time with an intense plea to angels and anyone watching to get us out of the river. I scanned the forest through the pouring rain and see no safe haven, no shelter, no place to go. I feel trapped in the car and notice the water lapping up the sides of the door and realize that if I was to open the door water would rush in. Sage sits quietly in the back watching the rainfall. Panic rises in my chest as my mind searches for the miracle I know we need. Images of being washed away swim across my mind's eye and in fear I turn to check that Sage is safe. He simply smiles at me. I take a deep breath and try the key again. The third turn of the key ignites the engine and I thankfully pull the car out of the water.

We are not safe yet as there are three fords to cross to get out of the forest. As I approach the third and final ford I ease the car to a halt before the rushing water. We are more than an hour into the forest, I have seen no cars, and this third ford looks deeper and the rushing of the water is menacing. My heart sinks as I realize that my low little hatchback is not going to make it through and I had pushed my luck as far as it will go. I close my eyes and send out a prayer as a flare into the forest, unsure if it will be heard or received. Moments later, a shadow forms down the road. A large four-wheel drive pulls up behind me followed by another. A man descends out of the high cab of the front vehicle and approaches the car. To me, he appears through the rain as an apparition. I wind down the window. He peers in and smiles at Sage.

"I am surprised you have made it this far," he says with a grin.

"My car stalled in the middle of the last two fords. I knew not to enter this one."

"No worries, we'll get you and your babe out. I'm going to pull in front of you and part the water, follow close behind me where the water will be the lowest. My mates in the second vehicle will follow you once they know you are safe."

That all sounded so easy and my mind relaxed with the knowledge that I was no longer alone in the forest. As he said, he pulled in front, parted the waters, and Sage and I swam on four wheels across the rushing divided waters. On the other side of danger the man waved me ahead. As I passed him, he gave me a thumbs up and I mouthed a thank you to him and his crew.

Out of the forest and down the highway Sage slept and I cried quietly. Once home I put us both in a hot bath and sat in the water feeling safe as I watched Sage splash with delight. The immense responsibility of caring for a young soul dripped off me into the bath. I thanked the angels, the crew of men in the vehicles, and all the magic and luck that had got us safely out of the forest. I marveled at the power of water and prayers. Both had amazed and shifted me as the forest drenched. Safe in the body of water, I reflected on the danger involved in the desperation of chasing, running, and seeking what is just out of your grasp. The image of Sage smiling at me from the back seat was strong and burnt into my memory. In the years that follow I learn again and again that water is a delight to Sage, and in water is one place outside his mind that he feels no fear. It was two days before Peter and Juzz made it out. They waited out the rain.

ON THE DAY SAGE TURNED ONE, I held a ceremony at the shore close to our new home. The sunset ceremony was as gentle as the water that day. A tree symbol was the central theme and represented those in our lives who keep us grounded like roots, and reaching for the sky like branches. Our tribe were acknowledged and Sage was celebrated. As I wrote the ceremony in the weeks before, the witch in me began to breathe again. Magic was woven and the moon was looked to for guidance.

We had survived our first year together. The journey north had served us well.

My babe crawled his way into walking and talking. My Sage, the little kid with a big heart. Sage was quirky, charming, silly, vulnerable, sweet and courageous. Sage was, I believe, a little old man hanging about in the body of a child. I remember one Sunday seeing him walk to the toilet with the cartoon section of the newspaper under his arm. My eyes were seeing a little boy but my heart and soul saw the shuffle of the little old man's feet.

As Sage grew so did my return and fascination with magic, healing, and the world unseen by eyes. I would share stories with Sage and together we would watch the moon. On the night of the full moon we often went moon hunting. We would wander the streets close to home seeking the full belly of light in the sky. I was able to see it first, but allowed Sage to be the hunter who would spot the glowing circle. One night Sage said:

"Mum, look there is the moon, and I am your sun."

I was deeply in love but also challenged in ways I never

had been. If Sage was the sun, I was the moon, if I was the yang, he was the yin. I like to be loud and stay out late, he liked the quiet and time alone. Early on, Sage learned that he needed his time and would often slip away. He would retreat into books or his favorite TV show and found time on his own to be his happy place. I would seek connection and sometimes be ignored or rejected. I would plan adventures and wish to be outdoors; he wanted the comfort of familiar walls. I would push and he would be still. We found moments of togetherness and I would treasure them. We told each other every day that we loved the other.

Love was present and pulsing in my mind as I tried in vain to seek my happy ever after. I believed that if I could create a family before Sage was old enough to miss one, then my sin of being the unwed mother and scarlet woman would be absolved. These thoughts, though unconscious, were the driving force behind my developing relationship with Mike. Mike was my best friend and Sage's godfather. We were high school buddies and had beyond school deepened our friendship. I remember one day in Biology class, grade 11, looking back at Mike and seeing in his eyes someone I knew. I didn't know it then but felt it, Mike and I are members of a soul family and have met each other more than once in lives we remember only in dreams.

Home north in Brisbane Mike and I spent a lot of time together. In that time, our friendship developed into love and my wish and desire drove us straight ahead down the road towards partnership. There was a lot of love, connection and genuine affection between Mike and I, and

Sage was deeply loved by us both. Our relationship shifted in a fast forward motion to living together and playing happy families. The pain and hurt felt by Shaun's lack of love, care, or concern festered under my skin and forced the narrative of the family. Love deepened and pressure built. We loved, we tried, we fought, we denied our truth, and a shady foundation was laid. I wanted the forever family, Mike fought his feelings of his role in Sage's life, and Sage simply went about the business of growing up. We honestly believed that we would make it and saw forever in our little family. Mike and I spoke of more children and in humor fought over names, we dreamed up a home we would one day buy together, and we loved Sage with all our might. My desired family had been created, but yet an itch was never satisfied and some days the scratching would tear at my skin. Happiness was one step away and forever hiding from sight. I couldn't find what I was missing.

ONE AFTERNOON ON A SET OF WOODEN STAIRS, sitting shaded from the sunshine, Sage and I played our version of *The Old Maid* card game. It's a card game for children that teaches about people and the characters of our world through matching pairs of the same card. The butcher matches the butcher and the old maid matches the old maid. If you get a match you win that hand. Sage and I never did play to win or compete with each other but we did love to play with the cards. We turned over each card for discovery and to learn, rather than to win. Each turn revealing a character; the baker, the policeman, the teacher. Sage had just turned four and was learning of the many roles people choose in life through the cards.

The witch card is turned over. "Look, Mum, it's you!" he declares with confidence.

I had never told him of my desire to be the white witch healer. He had played with toys as I studied my natural medicine modules when he was barely a crawling babe and into his toddler years. He had watched me leave for work to go to my clinic space where I had my own Chinese massage therapy and Reiki business. He had seen me treat people at home, and he had watched as I blended aromatherapy and flower essences into tinctures and balms. All of this happening in and around us, but it was never in my imaginings that he was taking any of this in, seeing what I was doing as the workings of a witch.

But he saw me as I wished to be seen. As the witch.

If I was a witch, Mike was the wizard. And Sage was our master teacher. We just didn't know it yet.

While Sage grew and learned to walk and talk, I furthered my desire to be a healer. I had graduated modules of study and had enough credit to begin practice as a massage therapist. One day at school I saw a note pinned to the bulletin board advertising a job at the "I Am Well Shop", a clinic close to the home I shared with Mike and Sage. I called the number in the hope it would be answered and would as I imagined, be the call that would help me to be well. In the reception space of the clinic, I sat opposite Krissy, with our matching small pointy noses and red lipstick, and felt at home. That day led me to the gift of the client list of the departing massage therapist and my spiritual learning took a turn up, out, and into the far reaches I had no knowledge of (yet). The clinic had three treatment rooms each filled on different days by a diverse range of practitioners, many of whom became my teachers. My soul sister relationship with Krissy was immediate and grew in strength as we navigated the possibilities of the soul and energy healing. Together we challenged and taught each other what we knew and discovered new realms of healing.

Our greatest lessons were in our workings with past lives, hypnosis, and Reiki healing. Through hypnosis under the guidance of Krissy, I saw myself as a healer over many lifetimes. I saw Sage as my soul brother who had protected me from an abusive father. I saw Mike and me, together in another life where he was a master with crystals and I was a teacher of many children. I saw Shaun- the man who had left me in many lifetimes – as the single, pregnant and alone woman. I saw myself in the three women who I saw in vision while laboring. I saw the threads of love that weave in and around our lives as we share time with our soul families. This is when I learned of the never-ending love and survival of the soul and its capacity to love and reach beyond lifetimes.

The day I saw Sage in hypnosis as my brother was deep and emotional. At the end of the hypnotic scene, Sage lay on his deathbed and as his sister, I swore to him that given the chance I would protect him the way he had protected me. A soul promise was made. That afternoon I took Sage to the park to play and marveled at his soul and our connection. Sage simply played and eased himself up and down the slide. I wondered if he knew and I was so happy I did. All upon a sudden, love seemed to make sense.

My desire to fall into my long lifeline as a healer twisted with my need to create a happy family. I dove deep and felt at purpose with the healing energy but separated from Mike. I teased him with stories in the hope it would tickle the wizard in him. I was ready to launch and wanted him with me. Mike chose to stay steady and not take flight. It felt like I had to choose. One night while out on a date I pleaded again with Mike to join me on the journey. I remember his response clearly.

"It's a lonely journey Deb."

I already felt alone and feeling lonely when with the one you love is a tortured feeling. Not immediately, but soon after that night and not long after Sage's fourth birthday, I packed up some belongings and moved Sage and me to my mother's house. My stitched together family was now breaking and over the next year, we broke. Sage retreated into TV and time with his Grandma; Mike drank beer and on varied odd days sought time with Sage; and I simmered in anger and denial of my actions that had led to the breaking point.

I committed to my healing practice and drove the many miles between my mother's house and the clinic and exhausted myself as my heart broke over and over. I was healing others and eroding with each treatment and mile. Months into this struggle I scraped together enough money to rent a small house close to the clinic. On the day Sage and I moved into The Little Green House, as we called it, I sat in the backyard with a new home filled with boxes, tired, smoking a cigarette, and questioning what I had done. Could I cope on my own? Was leaving Mike the best for me, for Sage? Is this my path? Will I be alone forever?

Sage trudged on heavy feet down the stairs that led to the garden. I was sure he was coming to ask me when we would be eating dinner as the sun was setting and the day had been long. Sage approached me and placed his hand on my shoulder.

"I'm proud of you Mum." A moment later Sage retreated back up the stairs and I sat in awe. Just when you begin to think the magic has gone it arrives with a hand gently on your shoulder. Sage's soulful way and insight into me straightened my spine and my resolve. For Sage, I would get up, and for Sage, I would move forward.

The time we spent at The Little Green House was marked by the first day of school. My little boy now wore a uniform, carried school books and was away from me five days a week until the school bell chimed and we could meet again to hug. Our rhythm shifted and slowly so did Sage.

I feared again I was the cause of the mess in his life and he would spend his adult years in therapy trying to make peace with why his mother had lost not one, but both fathers in his life. Mike moved into his own place close to The Little Green House and would be with Sage on the nights I spent working at the clinic. On the surface it looked like a great arrangement: I had a babysitter I trusted, Sage and Mike were able to spend time together, and we could all pretend we were getting on with life as the broken family. The catch was it became the norm for Mike to stay after I arrived home from work. Most nights we shared dinner, wine, and eventually my bed. We cruised through denial and I played with the possibility of a turn around of my happily ever after. Mike and I both knew we were playing with fire but neither one of us stepped away from the flame. One night, while drinking wine and sitting with Mike in the living room Sage stomped down the hallway. We were surprised to see him as we were sure he was asleep and in Dreamtime. He charged his way into the center of the room and declared: "Mike, you do not live here." And just as swiftly he left and put himself back to bed. We laughed at the silliness of being told off by a yet-to-turn five-year-old, but, as the days and nights passed I heard what Sage was actually saying. It was time to separate. I chose to listen and moved Sage and me away across the river and left my clinical practice, lover, and broken family on the far bank with no bridge. I chose Sage. It would be years before I had a healing room again.

ACROSS THE RIVER Sage did not seem happy, I was heart-broken and unhappy, and together we wallowed. I knew why I was in self-pity but was unsure as to why Sage's spirit was dampening. Sage's sense of himself and comfort in his body and soul took time to come to the light. School was hard. He became sad, turned to food for comfort, and retreated into his mind. The more I tried to tease him out, the more he disappeared. I had the sense I was missing something but could not place my finger on it. I wondered where the happiness of my child had gone. It was now glimpsed in moments when he was alone and lost in many moments in front of a screen.

Sage lived in his head and the imaginary world it created. He would tell me often that he had a very big brain and that message was given new weight when he was diagnosed with Aspergers Syndrome in the months before he turned six. The diagnosis was a shock at first but it did fill in the blanks and connect the dots. The habits of the little old man had meaning now: his self soothing, his retreat, his want to limit sound and smell, and his hate of school, parties and large gatherings.

On the day of the diagnosis, I asked the pediatrician how I explain all this to my almost-six-year-old son.

"Give it time. For now, he doesn't need to know anything is different. Things will change: your understanding of Aspergers, your attunement to his needs, the school will respond. You will know when he is ready to be told."

I wasn't so sure when or how that day would arrive but I was thankful for the days and weeks I was gifted as his mother to digest the news. The shock quickly turned to sadness and grief. Another twist in the anti-fairytale of my life. To me, this news was not welcome. A part of me was devastated.

Weeks later, one Sunday while laying in my bed reading, Sage came to ask me; "Mum, why am I different?"

"Everyone is different Sage, you are perfect exactly as you are." I rushed the words in an effort to appease him and return to my book and Sunday relaxation.

He left the room. Moments later he returned, with obvious frustration. "No. I am different. I am not the same as the others at school"

It was then that I got it. This was the moment the pediatrician had been talking about. "Sage, you have Aspergers. That's what makes you different."

"Aspergers. Okay." He left the room.

Moments later he returned with a curious gait. "So, what is Aspergers?"

"Aspergers means that you were born with a special brain. You see, feel and understand the world differently."

"So, my brain is special?"

"Yes Sage, You have been gifted a very special brain."

He skipped out of the room performing his 'Sage happy dance', a full-bodied sound and movement skip that looks and sounds like a horse in full joyful gallop.

In the days and weeks following, Sage happily announced to all those he came across that his name was Sage, which meant wise man, and he had been given a special brain. He was relieved to know his difference meant he was special and it seemed that maybe for the first time the world made sense to him. My devastation left and was replaced with relief that my son was delighted in his special brain and his world.

One day when Sage was six we were walking home from a stroll by the river. On the side of the road were a bunch of dandelions. Sage and I had a ritual of stopping at dandelions to make wishes.

"Sage, Dandelions! Let's stop." Sage and I both carefully chose which of the dandelions would be our wish maker. I went first.

"I wish for more money so I can take Sage on a grand adventure overseas."

I blew the wish and was hopeful that adventures beyond the river were in our future. Sage paused, kept his eyes focused on the flower and not on me. With little emotion Sage declared,

"I wish my mother would listen to me."

He blew his wish, discarded the stem and slowly walked towards home. I was taken aback. I thought we were having a lovely day. It took me years to realize that my lovely day was not always his. That to truly listen to Sage meant listening for what I did not expect, to meet him where he was at rather than inviting him to meet me. I did not always understand what Sage told me but I learned to sit longer and to simply listen. Over time his world became less of a strange place to me. It remained at times odd and seated in another dimension but it was his. As I softened to listen, Sage shared more.

Sage needed a solid foundation and in truth, so did I. The new reality of Aspergers was tricky to manage at first but became easy when I stopped to hear what Sage in silence was trying to tell me. I leaped again and gathered together the money to buy a house. I chose a small cottage home close to my mother, sister Sandra, and friend Justine, at Petrie in the outer suburbs of Brisbane. My soul cringed at the thought of a life in the suburbs but knew our lives needed to be close to those that loved us and that Sage needed a place to call home. In perfect alignment, the house I purchased was one street away from the school in the area that had a dedicated Special Needs Department. Sage found his sanctuary at school in the colored building with others who were 'different' and his life eased as school served his needs and cared for his special brain. Sage had new ground and I had a new garden. When we moved into the house the garden was overgrown with a wicked vine. Weeks and months into our new life in the suburbs I tore at the vine to reveal the beauty of the garden that lay dormant and trapped underneath the twisted green. As each new plant, shrub and tree were revealed it felt like a new possibility for Sage and I was emerging.

WHEN SAGE WAS EIGHT we traveled together to Spain on a holiday to see my friend Nina, her partner and their new son. In the plane, as it flew above the clouds Sage stared out the window in wonder. He turned to me and said, "Mum, I want to see the whole world." At that moment I wished to be the one who could grant that wish. I believed that we had enough time for many adventures and journeys. Beyond our trip to Spain, we would dream up the places we would go to. Most of our dreaming was done as we slowly walked to and from school. Sage had two places that he wished to visit: China and New York City. Sage could never explain why he wanted to go to China, but he was clear about his desire for New York City-he wanted to stay in the Plaza Hotel. I imagined that one day we may be there together.

The activation of positive thoughts was a lesson I taught Sage and one that became a constant in our lives. Sage had dreams and wished for their reality. I had manifestations I desired and wished for their potential. Our bigger dreams sat with us as we moved through the everyday and the positive thoughts were often centered upon everyday things. We would add positive energy to the book we wanted to borrow from the library and were delighted when it was there. We sent positivity to people we knew who were challenged and hoped the best for them, and Sage spent a lot of time sending positive thoughts to his latest desire, often the new Lego set he had seen at the toy store he was hoping I would buy.

Sage took positive thoughts very seriously. To activate he would clench his eyes and fists shut and focus his thoughts and his desired intention. One day I dared to ask him a question when he was in activation mode. I got in a lot of trouble that day. Sage huffed, told me his positive thoughts needed silence, and turned again to his task. I didn't dare to interrupt his positive thoughts again. Over time I saw that most of what he wished for came to him. Sage was never surprised as it was what he was expecting.

He was close to turning nine when he began to identify as the inventor and his life gathered momentum. The little old man who had methodically been growing and learning found his passion and his imagination took flight. Sage's quirky personality now had a channel and his brain shifted into high gear. Long detailed stories of his inventions were told repeatedly and the design of his inventor lab was carefully crafted.

As Sage and I balanced into each other our roles would sometimes shift. Sage was a serious lad who did not like to make mistakes and was sure with each step. Me, not so much. Sage was the one to lecture me about my drinking and would inquire with a stern glare if I really needed to attend the event or gathering on a school night. If I pulled the car into the drive-through liquor store he would side glance at me and mumble, "Wine again, huh?" I often felt like a teenager under the guise of a disapproving parent. If Sage sensed that my party needs were revving up he would simply ask, "Mum, can you please take me to Grandma's?" The mother in me always made sure he was comfortable and cared for, and the cheeky witch in me often flew off to the party.

The one party Sage wished to attend was Halloween. His beloved cartoons were filled with stories of costumes and trick or treat adventures, and they were all American. It was 2011 and Halloween was slowly dripping into Australian culture as the television sets in homes poured out the delight of the stories to expectant and wanting children. Sage would ask me for very little, so when he asked if we could go trick or treating I took notice. I was wanting to meet his desire but knew that no-one on our street would be decorating, adorning costumes or filling bowls with candy. Our street was small with less than ten houses and other than a baby and a toddler next door there were no other children. Sage in determination would not let his Halloween wish evaporate and coaxed me into an exploration of possibilities. Sage's positive thoughts and determination won as we settled on a plan that could possibly work. Together we wrote a note to each house on our street. It read something like this…

Hello, this is Sage from number 6. I will be celebrating Halloween this year. At Sunset on the 31st in costume, with my mum, I will be trick or treating up and down the street. If you would like to join the Halloween fun and invite me to your door please leave your outside light on. I promise to only go to the homes with the light on. Thank you, Sage.

I felt nervous as Halloween approached and in an attempt to avoid hurt feelings I purchased bags of candy and hid them in the house. On the night of Halloween

Sage dressed as Ironman, his favorite character. I dressed as a witch (obviously) and my sisters Liz, Sandra, cousin Bayley, and Grandma costumed up and joined in on the fun. As we hit the street my face spread wide into a grateful smile as I saw almost all the lights in our street were on. Sage skipped into his happy dance and set out to knock on the first door. That night Sage bought the street alive with magic as each door was opened. Our neighbors played along with tricks and treats and one woman, who lived alone and was mostly quiet and unseen, answered the door in full costume, dressed as a witch, complete with broom and hat.

That evening reminded me that as children do, adults also wish for magic and play. To Sage, the magic lay just under the surface. It could be forgotten by me as he played quietly in his mind. His vibration was forever creating and believing. He was just one solution and positive thought away from all he needed.

IN OUR DAYS TOGETHER IN PETRIE, Sage would invite me to sit on the couch. "Why?" I would ask "Is there something you need?" The need was stillness. Over time we met each other more and more on the couch. I was learning. We had a red couch and would make appointments with each other to spend time on the couch. I learned to love our time on the red couch. If I was lucky, the appointment made was for a big squeezy hug. The big squeezy hug was a specialty of Sage's. Sage spent most of his time in imagination and his reality of life as a famous inventor. He memorized, calculated, created, and designed. His mind was his playground. The world outside his mind was a confusing and sometimes hurtful place. The big squeezy hugs helped Sage to stay connected to the earth and connected to me. Sage didn't understand social language and the world continued to ask him to be social. He would become anxious and overstimulated and learned early on to seek time on his own. The wise old man chose when to enter and when to retreat. As his mother, I was aware of his struggle and acknowledged his resilience and courage. At times I was saddened by the little effort that was made to meet him in his world. I would try but the truth is, I never really understood what was happening in his world. It seemed so strange to me. I imagine just as strange as we were to him.

Sage's wild creative imagination landed in a world of technology and future visions. In Sage's world, he was already a famous inventor and to him, his imaginings were real. For Sage it was simply a case of waiting to grow up before his dream became his everyday reality. He would share with me the details of the new design for his inventor lab he would build one day, with a room on the side for me so I could visit. He would draw intricate images of shapes and contours that to him meant something. He would play with columns of numbers and often ignore the homework task to flip to the back of his school book where his secret math equations were documented. One day, when I spotted him in rows of numbers rather than homework, I asked him what he was doing. "Nothing. You wouldn't understand," he said as he quickly flipped back the page to conceal his magic making of numbers.

As nine clicked over to turning ten, his dream of being a famous inventor became a fixation and an everyday desire. He became so attached to the dream that I began to fear for him. His dream felt so close to impossible and he was so attached that I feared his heart was set to be broken. I gently began to question the dream, trying to make space for reality to settle. And each time I was met by answers and possibilities from Sage. He believed in his dream, without a doubt, he was a famous inventor – just a very short one. So I let go. I let go of the fear and in that moment I became the mother of a famous inventor!

I surrendered to the suburbs, to being a single parent, to loving Sage exactly as he was, and I began to hope and breathe life into a new version of happily ever after. I transformed the spare room into a healing space and began to see clients and give healings. I felt at home again after a long time away. I wished for an opening of my heart. I felt ready for more love.

And then a sharp shift of energy swept in and ripped at my heart. What I discovered is a broken heart can never be closed. An open heart, even one that has been smashed to pieces invites magic and sees layers of wonder in everyday things. The ordinary became extraordinary.

IN THE EARLY WEEKS and months of 2013, I knew something was wrong and so did Sage. Something had shifted or was shifting. I often found myself holding my breath. One evening I was sitting at my desk working and Sage came to me. I expected him to ask me for food or permission to watch TV, but instead, he said:

"Mum, I have been wondering all day if maybe it would be better if I didn't exist at all."

My heart broke a little more. Days before I had found him standing out on the street in the pouring rain. When I asked him what he was doing he said:

"I need to be punished."

"For what Sage? You have done nothing wrong."

For what he could not say. I asked him further about the need for punishment and he shared that he had been punishing himself for some time. One punishment was to wake in the night. He conjured up a reality where it was decided he did not deserve a bed. He would make himself sleep the rest of the night on the floor. I never knew as Sage always rose before me. My mind flashed with images of self-flagellation as practiced by fanatics in search of redemption. What the fuck was happening to my son? Why was this happening, and why now? When I asked further about his feelings and thoughts of punishment he would hold his head in frustration and tell me his brain was telling him things and making him feel crazy. Sage had no answers as to why he felt the way he did and I too had no idea what had changed. Was this a side to Sage's experience of Aspergers that was new to us? Or was it something different?

In the mornings, I would run. I often thought – am I running towards or running away? I felt stuck in time and space, yet moving. I simply had no idea where I- or we – were headed. As I ran in those days and weeks before Sage died I would hear a repeated message. *"Go to where the water flows."* Was that for me? Or for another? Am I running towards or running away? And water… what water?

The shift taking place was heavy and felt like it was dragging me down below the water line. I was close to drowning in the unknown. I tried to stay above the water but did not always succeed. I have a clear memory of one night. A glass of wine in hand, I was on the living room floor howling, sobbing and drowning. The wine was serving as my self-soothing medication and released by the end of the bottle the river of anguish I had been trying to hide from my son. Sage sat on the red couch and watched silently as I sobbed.

I began to pick up the pieces. Appointments with our family doctor and mental health practitioners were made, referrals filled. I spent time with family exploring options and talking with his teachers to get advice. Sage hated it. He didn't know how to talk about what was happening. I didn't know the right questions to ask. One day as we drove to yet another appointment with yet another professional who was supposed to be able to help us make sense of what was shifting I spoke to Sage about why we were trying, what we were seeking.

"Sage, do you know why we need to keep going to these appointments?"

"I don't want to talk about it," he replied, holding his gaze out the window.

This was a common response. Sage didn't feel the need to talk about most things, except his inventions, his favorite TV show, or what we were having for dinner (he loved to eat!). I had learned to balance my questioning and 'mum talk' with silence, but this day was begging for some 'mum talk'.

"Sage, I want the best for you. The best possible life, to be as happy as you can be. Sometimes people need help to sort out their thoughts and feelings so they can find happiness. This is not about you being broken or wrong, it's about finding your happiness. These appointments are our way of searching for what will help you to be happy."

There was something in this that Sage heard and understood. He turned his gaze and began to open up. He shared his fear of being crazy and different, his lack of understanding of what the adults wanted him to be or do, his desire to be happy and his forever dream of becoming a famous inventor. I listened and he felt heard. I began to believe that we were going to make it. Surely, somewhere soon the solution to Sage's feelings and negative thoughts would be found and we would be okay. I kept telling myself this. It was not in my imagining that I was again preparing for death.

IN FEBRUARY OF 2013, my Uncle Barry passed away. He was my father's only brother; another Driscoll man was gone. His exit felt like a rumble of the earth. Shortly after he was laid to rest, my sister Kath was diagnosed with breast cancer. The dominos of the Driscoll family began to fall. I thought the domino for Sage and I had already fallen. It felt that way.

Little did we know that the year of 2013 asked the Driscoll clan to draw straws. We were all to be challenged and changed and our core was to be shaken. I didn't know it then but Sage was to draw the shortest straw.

With my sister's diagnosis, we were drawn south to the Blue Mountains west of Sydney to be with her, to Wentworth Falls – a place where the water flows. Sage loved the mountains. I spent time in the mountains when I was pregnant and over the years we'd holidayed there. Sage would often ask me when we would be going to the mountains again and when I asked him why he would simply say he liked it there.

I did not feel a sense of flow with our decision to journey south to the mountains. I felt fear and it lay unsettled for days. I knew we needed to go but I knew that something was wrong. In distress one day while making plans for the journey I told my mother that I feared that we would journey to the mountains and one of us would not return. When the words came rushing out of my mouth I knew them to be true. The fear was palpable – it was in the room, had pulled up a seat, and was making itself very comfortable. I tried to push away the truth and decided I was simply over emotional with all that had been happening with Sage and now my sister's diagnosis.

It felt like I had no choice but to journey south and move forward so I decided to bury my fear, strap on my smile and make the trip a fun holiday for Sage. My mum, Sage, my sister Liz and I, travelled together from Brisbane. My sister Heather was also traveling to the mountains from Melbourne. We would all be together. Sage loved long journeys. He would retreat into his mind and dream of his elaborate inventions which I never really understood, but were created with great detail. On the trip Sage was happy and all seemed well. It appeared that fear had not come along for the ride.

While at a hotel mid-journey I received a message in a dream that was vivid and felt like it had its own pulse. Was it a dream or had I received a visitor in the night? Just before dawn a spirit guide sat on the edge of the bed I was sleeping in with Sage. He was tall, thin, of Middle Eastern descent, and looked about 50 years old. He wore a very elaborate hat that made him look like he had some kind of authority. He said to me:

"I know you do not want to hear this as you have forgotten each morning the nights I have come to visit, but please listen as this is the last time I can come. We are running out of time. What you need to remember is *the research is important.*"

I woke knowing that this message had weight but I had no idea what it meant. I was doing a masters degree at the time and concluded it was a spirit affirmation of my research. I also knew that this was not correct. My heart knew the message was pointing me in a new direction. I simply had no idea where.

In the mountains Sage was content. He spent time with his cousins, his aunts, and his Grandma. He gleefully indulged in a movie marathon with Harry Potter and magic. He read books with his Aunt Kath, and on his last night he devoured apple crumble (apples were his delight!) specially made for him by Aunt Heather and Aunt Liz. He went to his bed happy, joking with his grandma, knowing he was loved.

That night, sometime in the darkness, I woke. I was on a mattress in the spare room with two sisters sleeping on either side of me. Sage was in the next room also on a mattress sleeping next to his Grandmother, who as our Elder, won the luxury of the bed. Unable to get up without disturbing my sisters I lay awake unsure of what had woken me but very aware of a strange feeling I could not identify. At some point I slept again. The next morning one by one the family woke. Sage was not with us which was strange as he almost always rose early. The only time he slept late was when he was unwell. I decided he needed rest and let him sleep. We didn't know then that he had already gone.

Sometime in the darkness of the night his spirit had slipped away.

Children's bedtime prayer

Now I lay me down to sleep,
I pray the lord, my soul to keep.

If I should die before I wake,
I pray the lord, my soul to take.

My mother often said this prayer to Sage. She was taught this prayer by her mother, Sage's great grandmother.

PART THREE
On My Way Home

The Compass points South.
The way of the birds at winter and the deeper shadow of
our soul.

The Element of Fire.
Creation, Destruction and Transformation.

Full Moon.
The fullness of a lesson and all sides can be seen.
Personal growth, spiritual development and
magical insight.

OVER THE YEARS, alone in bed late at night, unable to sleep, I had more than once written a eulogy for Sage in my mind. The repeated ritual of insomnia began to take shape. I would appreciate and acknowledge his grandmother and godmother for their love and support, I would share stories of his kindness and vulnerability, and I would thank Daniel and David for always being his friends. Other nights I felt compelled to sneak into his room to check that he was still breathing. I had taken this as a crazed act of fear mongering. Now I wonder: was I preparing all this time? Had I been warned? Was my soul self-protecting and preparing me for this shift, the one that will never melt away?

I had listened and had gone to where the water flows. I had heard the spirit guide on his last visit. I had felt the fear and tightening of time. I opened my heart to the unknown and was being gently directed to where I did not want to go. To the death day of my son.

THE DAY WAS BEGGING TO BEGIN so I went to the room where Sage lay. There was no disturbance in the sheets. No sign of distress. It was only when I felt his cold hands and saw the light in his eyes gone did I know that I had missed the exit. I never knew a soul could scream until mine did. "SAGE" I screamed again and again. One by one family members flood the room and screaming fills the small space. Sage is swiftly moved off the mattress and our family friend, Sarah, also staying with us, begins CPR. I cry and watch. My mind repeats: He is gone and it is too late. I had seen the blood markings of still death on his body and his toes were pointed in the way only a corpse can do. I remember seeing these markings on Nick's body as he sat dead in the passenger seat. The CPR looked violent on his small body and my screaming shifted to yelling: "Leave him alone, don't touch him, don't hurt him."

Somewhere in the confusion someone had called an ambulance. As the officers hurriedly entered the room everyone stood back. I sat by Sage. A heart monitor was strapped to his chest and we waited out the moments it took to show there was no heartbeat. The ambulance officer gently met my eyes. Time slowed down to the point of stillness. Keeping me locked with his eyes the officer pointed to the empty screen.

"I am so sorry. There is no heartbeat. He is gone."

With the confirmation I not only screamed, I flew. My body lurched across the room and thrashed with an agony groan from deep within. The bruise on my leg I inflicted from banging into the furniture was deep and dark for days, it was the only way I knew my body had flown.

When the ambulance officers left and the screaming had ended, I began to pray. The horror quietened down and a sense of peace settled. I lay next to Sage and I allowed my heart to open up towards heaven. Sage was on a direct flight home to our spiritual maker, and my dad, and our soul family. He was gone and I could not bring him back so I followed what my spirit whispered through the shock. I opened my broken heart and prayed. My prayers were not to God or any figure in particular, they were to Sage and who I hoped was on the other side to meet him. I called out to my father to meet my son. I say prayers. Some may say the mad ravings of a mother's heart.

It didn't take long for the police to arrive. As it was not known why or how Sage had died the room was to them an active crime scene. They told me I would have to leave. "Hell NO!" was my sharp reply. I was not met by any resistance. Sadness lay heavy in the officers eyes. One of them stepped forward and said. "Okay, but only you. And you can't move anything." The officers took turns watching guard and the room transformed into a sacred space. It felt to me like the passing of Sage's soul was being protected.

We waited for the detectives from Sydney, two hours away, to come to take photos and to complete reports. As the only one allowed in the room I was grateful to have time with Sage, to be with his body to pray, to sing in whispers, and to tell him bedtime stories. I held his body as a way to hold on. Something in me knew that he was okay. I believe that angels will not take you until it is your time. How I had learned this or decided it was true was lost to me, but I held onto the idea as my lifeline in the wake of my son's death.

Later in the day the detectives and photographers arrived and then left again. The guard of the room was lifted and my family was allowed and invited in. Sage had time with us all and I invited my mother to lead us in prayer. In unison and in whispers we chanted the familiar words of the Our Father prayer followed by Hail Mary. The final line of the Hail Mary prayer sealed our sorrow. "Now and at the hour of our death."

All too soon for me the hearse arrived to take his body away. I stood outside the room so they could lift Sage onto the gurney that would take him away. As Sage left his resting place and was rolled down the hallway one of the police officers on guard grabbed me in an embrace to turn me away from his passing body. In a vulnerable and human moment the officer collapsed into me and sobbed. For that moment, I was holding him and the mother in me was thankful I was given someone to hold.

The afternoon was spent making calls announcing death and at the police station giving statements and signing papers. Shock settled in. The evening was spent in stunned silence, among my family, looking out to the trees and gulping rivers of wine.

I found out the next day that Sage was not coming home with me. Emily from the Coroner's office called to tell me the autopsy had told them next to nothing. I cried in disbelief, with a hint of guilt and anger. What had happened to my son?

"There is one thing that is abnormal. Do you want to know?" Emily said.

"Yes, please. Anything you know."

"The only information that points to something that the initial report cannot determine, is that Sage's brain is larger than the average size of a ten year old boy."

I laughed. "Sage knew that. He told me that often – that he had a very big brain."

I gave permission for further examination and tests. Sage needed to stay and I needed to go – to go home without him. I was told further results may take up to twelve months and testing a brain post-life is a task that reaps little reward and often no findings, but it was the only option. I needed to know what had happened to my son. The mystery settled into my soul and I released into the unknowing.

ONE NIGHT, days after Sage had passed, I dreamt of him. We saw each other in the dream space and ran into an embrace. We were so happy to see each other. I was holding my son and my heart was beating again in joy. In that dream I heard Spirit tell me that this was the best way: for me to be left without him – as I was the mother and stronger and this way meant that he was not left without me. I awoke feeling thankful that my son did not have to feel the pain I was experiencing.

AS I TRAVELLED DOWN THE MOUNTAIN towards the airport I became numb. It felt like the world around me was carrying on with its turning but I was frozen. Numb soon transformed into guilt as I was sure I was meant to be feeling something. The mother who had lost her child only yesterday was surely supposed to be full of feeling. So numb became guilt, and so I drank. Wine was necessary and not sipped but gulped. I drank at the airport bar and then the whole flight home. By the time our plane landed in Brisbane I was drunk and had become delirious. My sisters, Heather and Elizabeth, also drunk, were delirious with me. The smallest thing seemed funny. I guess we were laughing to stop the tears from taking over. My mother was silent. It all felt surreal and then after touchdown very real again. In the car driving towards home I let my eyes close to seek numb again. The wine helped to ease me into a lull as the passing lights of the highway blurred the road home.

When we arrived at my house I announced to my sisters and mother that I would be going in alone. If I couldn't bring Sage home then no one was coming home with me. My irrational hope was, if I was alone maybe I would be closer to my son. All I found was empty rooms. My drunken stumble led me to Sage's room. The smell was familiar, the toys and books well worn and strewn around, the colours bright as a young child's room should be. I sat on his bed and waited for my expected sadness and tears but was shaken by a rage that propelled my feet to fly. In an unconscious strike I kicked the pedestal fan and felt satisfied when it hit the floor with a clang. I stomped my heavy, drunk feet through the house and stopped in the back room at Sage's desk. I picked up a chair at his desk and threw it into the backyard. That felt good. I walked into the kitchen and my glaring eyes sought out the breakable items. I stopped frozen in a moment of clarity through the haze. "No Debra, put yourself to bed." Knowing no good could come of the day you fly home without your son, I staggered to my room and passed out.

IN THE MORNING I woke with a heavy heart and a sore head. With coffee in hand, I stared at the chair in the backyard. I stared into the garden for I don't know how long, but long enough to realise I had a choice. I descended the five wooden stairs into the garden and picked up the chair. I went to Sage's room and picked up the fan. I walked from room to room. I was alone in a home that was now without heart. It was like walking through the skeleton left behind after the decay of flesh makes its way to completion. I was left with the remains of a life I had built and the bones that show a body was once here.

It was time to open and fill the spaces between the bones. I knew that now more than ever I needed to lean on Spirit and those I loved. If I closed in now, it was possible I may never open again. So I sent out word and opened my home. I invited everyone who knew and loved Sage and they all came. They came bearing their gifts. I centred myself and began to receive. Years later, I learnt that I had in my own way "called the sitting of Shiva," a Jewish week-long death ritual that follows the burial of a relative in the home they inhabited. My garden version of sitting Shiva was the constant flow of people, food, wine, tears, connection, laughter and stories of Sage.

As my fascination with Spirit, magic and healing continued beyond my twenties and deepened in my thirties, I had come to rely upon my sense of intuition, my belief in angels, the power of the universe and believed we were all connected – not just in this life but in lives before and beyond. My studies in natural healing practises and my lived experience as a Reiki Master shaped my spiritual practice. Teaching Reiki, using oracle cards for guidance, and the practice of meditation and affirmation had become my norm and I relied upon them to help me navigate life. I wondered as I sat on the kitchen floor, where I had landed when my legs collapsed under the heaviness of shock and the early waves of grief, how this would play into this new chapter of my life. How much would my spiritual practice help me? It was no longer time to study or teach, it was time to apply. A quiet yet present part of me feared that it would not be enough and despite effort I would still drown under the weight of grief. I became not only curious but felt a responsibility to find again the silver lining. I reminded myself that death comes bearing gifts.

Justine was the first to arrive. "What will happen now?" she asked.

I didn't know the answer but I knew everything had changed and would never be the same again. I glimpsed a moment in my future. A time when I would be okay again. It felt like life was to be re-assigned, re-imagined and re-defined. But not yet. Now the time asked for me to sit and to be. To be with the knowing that my son had died.

It took much longer than I expected for the shock of Sage's death to align with my soul and settle. Grief, in her full presence, did not arrive for days and her lessons were not felt for weeks, some taking years. In the days that followed Sage's death I felt both numb and inspired by love and magic, a very strange mix.

I sat for days in my garden and home and watched as

it filled with love, grief, care and kindness. It is difficult to remember details. I remember being thankful that I was not alone. I was surrounded by many friends and my family. Julie, Mardi and Nina had all flown to be in the garden with me. I remember being aware of the many amazing and generous people in my life. I remember more than once finding my legs could not hold me and I was again with death on the floor holding my knees, sometimes crying and sometimes just simply unable to stand. Over and over again to those who arrived, I told the story of Sage's passing. In the re-telling it appeared to be a narrative of the perfect death of the wise old man. "He died peacefully in his sleep."

IN THE LIVING DAYS, on weekends, Sage and I would go to the local trash 'n' treasure to collect old pieces of technology: computers, typewriters, printers, anything with parts. He would then delight in taking the technology apart with his trusted tools. Each part revealed another knowing and new lessons in how the technology of the world worked. Every part extracted was kept. This was Sage's inventor business, that was to him, imperative to his development and to him, something that a mere "normal" person like me would never understand. To Sage, this was his magic and he took it very seriously. Over time the pieces developed into a large collection.

On the day of the opening of my garden I built a large spiral in the garden with pieces of Sage's technology. The centre piece was an old vinyl turntable. The spiral spun out to create what I hoped to be a portal. My wish was the beloved technology would invite Sage's spirit into the garden. I desperately wanted him there. The spiral gave me hope that his spirit would float down to be with me, with us.

I had said more than once the garden of that home saved my soul and it was now the place my soul and heart lay open. In the corner stretched the large Jacaranda tree I had blessed and loved. The Jacaranda tree was the Queen of the garden. She was obviously old, amazingly large and wore her purple flowers that bloomed in September like a majestic bejeweled crown. To reach her you walked to the deepest left corner of the garden. There she stood tall, proud and wide, with three low thick branches that naturally split to create a wooden seat of earth magic, a throne.

I learnt early on to not sit on her throne despite its allure. When I did dare to ease my simple non-Queen self upon her she would groan. Quietly at first. If I stayed and tried to settle she would raise her wood tone and simply say, "Get Off." Her warning was clear and her command was always honored.

Sage and I lived in that home for more than three years and in that time my relationship with the garden and the Queen grew. I learned to respect that I was uninvited upon the throne but under her canopy was a place I was allowed. I landscaped her feet and field beyond into my ritual space. I lay bark, planted flowers, bought outdoor candles and added my own throne – an old discarded wooden bench. It became my retreat, a place to be with my thoughts, to wish upon magic and to dream my way away from the reality of a single mother thrown on purpose into the deep suburbs. Sage very rarely came under the tree and if ever he did it was by invitation or his desire to have a need met. "Mum, when are you coming in to make dinner? It's getting dark."

I began by sitting there. Under her, I felt safe. I deeply appreciated how little she spoke and felt the ease of not having to report to her how I was. As my whole self took a breath under my Queen, I heard a new message.

"I know God won't give me anything I can't handle. I just wish he didn't trust me so much"

Why this quote rang in my ears was a mystery, but one I heard. And it raised the question: where was God in all of this?

On the Sunday of the first weekend without Sage, my brother bought his children to my garden. My niece, Tara, who is only months younger than Sage gave me a picture.

"I don't know why Aunty Deb but I wanted to draw this picture for you."

I looked at the picture and saw the face of my spirit guide, Cassandra.

"I know why Tara."

Years before, through meditation, I had asked to be introduced to my spirit guide. The image shown to me in meditation was a woman with masses of fiery red hair and I was told, her name is Cassandra. In my bedroom I had two images of her – one from an artist based in the Blue Mountains and one painted by my sister Liz. I took Tara into my room to show her Cassandra. I hugged her and thanked her for bringing me this very special message. Cassandra was with me. Was this my evidence of God? Tara was delighted and impressed with her ability and gift and I delighted in her pleasure – for a moment. And then I remembered that no more pleasure of Sage could be hugged, so I hugged Tara tighter followed promptly by the pouring of more wine.

I felt my spirit strengthen to the task. Rituals and ceremonies were needed. Decisions needed to be made. My mind had left, my body mostly numb, my heart broken, but my spirit felt strong. I knew the seeds I planted now would grow for years so I wished the best for myself. Remembering my vow from my early twenties to fully meet and feel grief when she arrived next I promised myself three things. I would wish the best for myself. I would go through the centre of the grief – not under, not over, but through and, I would commit to go to the scary places if they presented as the best or only way forward.

I purposely stayed connected to those with me as a way to stay stable and of this earth. My spirit sought the centre of the garden-technology spiral and I was often lost in my wanderings of mind and soul as my heart reached up to heaven. I am not sure what those around me saw but I felt split between heaven and earth. I was again very much alive but not sure I wanted to be.

My creative companion Hayley was charged with writing and officiating Sage's memorial. My sister Liz stepped in to assist with her creative talents. Nina, who had flown in from Spain, ensured everyone was invited. Godmother Julie set to task in the garden and together with her brother, built a ceremonial fire pit that was cement-sealed by Justine, Nina, and Sage's friends Daniel and David. Mardi fed everyone good food and Anna hung ceremonial grief flags, a symbol of Sri Lanka.

My family came and went. My sister Sandra managed the comings and goings of people and donations. My brother managed the arrangements with the funeral director. Kath flew north from the mountains. Heather told the neighbours of the fire to be lit the night of the memorial. Judith gathered photos and created the visual story of Sage in a large photo album. Liz created with Hayley. My mum was with me.

The school called. Friends arrived and left and arrived. There was constant activity. I drank a lot and ate only a little. I wondered what others saw in me. Was I doing this right? Are these the correct actions of a grieving mother? The rain came and went.

I would wait for more than two weeks for Sage's body to come home, to see him again, to dress him for his final rest. To place him in the coffin and to kiss him goodbye. I knew that it was very unlikely that I would ever know what had happened to my little boy. I released and set to task in the celebration of Sage. It was time to write the eulogy. Would I pull out my prepared spiel of my son's life? How the fuck do you do this?

I had the journal I had written for Sage when he was in my belly and in the early years following I had written him one or two letters a year. I had written to share with him our life stories and to ensure that his early life was documented. One afternoon, in preparation for the eulogy, I chose to read the journal and letters. I sat myself under the Jacaranda tree at the back of the garden. I expected to read stories of my son but what was revealed were stories of the mother of the son. It was all about me and how I felt as his mother. Only a few stories of Sage were found in the letters. I was horrified. I saw myself reflected on the page as a woman in pain. Had I screwed up my son? Was I to blame for the absence of his father? My agony and loneliness as a single parent unsure at every step. The desired fairytale of my life had twisted to reveal bitterness, pain and guilt – the anti-fairytale. I sat in this discomfort under the Jacaranda tree. How much had I missed while I tumbled in the muck? Flashes of Sage over the years caring little for the muck and simply getting on with life and love played before my eyes. All my worry had been for nothing. All it had done was take me away from moments in time. Moments I had with Sage.

A steady resolve rose. Sage and his story were to be central and celebrated at his memorial.

ON THE DAY OF THE MEMORIAL I woke early. I felt lost and knew the only way to be found was to seek the trees. I drove to the river and wandered aimlessly among the open spaces between the trees. My body was pulled towards the bank of the river and I sat to watch her flow. The pull to go deeper persisted so I edged closer and slid my body down the muddy bank. I could not seem to get close enough so I entered her and stood with the water lapping at my thighs. That afternoon I was to stand in honour of my son. The eulogy was mine to share. I asked the river how I could possibly do this. She simply said: "Allow it to flow." I was not satisfied so asked again. The river fell silent and simply flowed. I did not feel ready or able. I crawled out of the river, now a mess of water and mud.

As I made my way through the trees I saw a woman walking directly towards me. We were the only two in the park. Unlike me she was neat, with her hair pulled back, and a pep in her step. As we passed she smiled at me. I was drawn to the colours on her shirt and saw her shirt had a message printed on it: "I've got sparkle". Yes, that is the piece I needed! Just a little bit of sparkle. Today was the day my son was to be celebrated and damn straight, he deserved sparkle.

The sky clouded over and heavy rain came. I agreed with the sky. I also wanted to cloud over and cry. But this day asked for sparkle. I dressed in a dark long dress with a splash of red, and felt like I was putting on a costume. I was driven to the ceremony by my friend Steve and in the company of Godmother Julie. The rain poured. I wondered how my mother was. I saw fear sitting in the back seat next to Julie. I had no idea how I was to do this, to walk into this. I asked fear to fuck off, invited sparkle to enter, and held on tight to Julie and Steve. As we arrived the rain began to ease. The site was filled with red balloons, children, friends, family, and a strange sense of celebration. The sense memory of Sage strengthened my spine and my heart opened.

The memorial was by the water in the same place where, years before, I had led our community through Sage's first birthday ceremony. So many people had gathered. People I loved had travelled from far and away, so many others surprising me with their presence. I was overwhelmed by the expansive crowd of people. The rain had not kept the mourners away. The scene was set and decorated with a splash of red. Red was Sage's favourite color and the invitation had requested people wear red. Sage was everywhere and nowhere. The technology spiral from the garden had been transported to the ceremony site, I was hoping it would draw Sage to us. I so wanted him to be there.

The celebration of Sage began. The sky cleared and the rain stayed away.

The ceremony, written by Hayley, celebrated Sage's eleven gifts: Love, Strength, Imagination, Talent, Laughter, Reverence, Generosity, Compassion, Dreams, Gratitude, and Courage.

Laughter mixed with tears and an awesome young man was remembered and honoured.

My friend Beth sang one of my favourite songs, *The River is Flowing*.

The river is flowing, flowing and growing
The river is flowing down to the sea

Mother, the river is flowing, flowing and growing
The river is flowing down to the sea

Mother carry me, your child I will always be
Mother carry me, down to the sea

Family, friends and Sage's teachers shared stories and prayers. I shared my eulogy and Sage, The Famous Inventor, was acknowledged and applauded. Godmother Julie and my Mother were honored for the big part they had played in Sage's life, my family was acknowledged for their love and support, and Daniel and David were thanked.

At the end of the memorial the Driscoll family stood in a circle of honor and strength around the technology spiral. My friends Ariel and Rex played their drums and a pulse charged over the beach. It was over. I felt devastated and strong. Champagne began to flow.

For Sage

*In a magical moment that is to last 10 years and 11 months,
worlds collide
The old school and the new age meet and merge
The little old man arrives*

Arriving exactly on time

*Beginning with peace and ease the little old man settles
into the body of a child
Sage Joseph Driscoll is born*

*Working together in time and space
Working together in love and light
The little old man and the child begin to craft the dream
The dream of the famous inventor*

*I have a very big brain he would tell me
And I am a famous inventor*

*Holding on tight to his dreams, Sage created a world
A world where possibilities are endless and the potential of
his brain was to be explored*

*I love you a lot he would tell me
As he grounded down into the earth and into me*

*In a magical moment that lives deep in the night
Worlds collide and my child leaves*

Leaving me exactly too soon

Love Mum

LATER THAT EVENING, back home in my garden, the ceremonial fire for Sage was lit. The drums bellowed and again I felt my spirit grow in strength. I was so happy for Sage and proud of my son. If only he had been here to see it. To see how many had gathered. To hear his lessons shared publicly. To bear witness to the honouring of his life. I wondered where he was. Was he there? I had to believe so. Sage was dead and I was very much alive. With just a little sparkle.

Time warped after that night. The celebration had been full but now my garden emptied. It was not over yet. Sage's body was not home. I noted the moon. Sage had died on the last quarter of the moon as she was waning. The memorial was on the new moon auguring a new reality and now the moon began to ease towards fullness. I did not know what the full moon would reveal but knew she was growing and as she did it felt like the waters were rising.

In the first quarter of the moon the school held a ceremony. My mother joined me and we all gathered at the oval for a tree planting. Sage's classmates had drawn pictures and written him letters. The tree was planted with the gifts from his classmates wrapped up and surrendered into the turned up soil. I stood there full of feelings for the children. Just before the Easter break one of their classmates had lost a mother to cancer. They left on holidays already in relationship to death, to return to school with one of their own gone. How does a ten year old understand this I wondered. As the ceremony was wrapping up I felt compelled to speak to the children. I spoke of kindness, of taking care of each other, and believing in their dreams. I thanked those who had taken the time to care for Sage as he navigated life at school. I wished them well and felt a deep desire to hug and care for them all.

Time further warped as the moon waxed. It felt to me like my costume was still on as the moon was filling. My son was not yet laid to rest and until he was I was to hold vigil. To remain in costume. To stay in prayer. And on the days I could manage, add just a little bit of sparkle. Most days I sought the company of the river and trees. With them I could surrender to my grief and feel held by them. I was a mother without a child to care for. I had been set free. I felt guilt at feeling the freedom and grief at feeling my loss.

In the quieter moments of the early days and weeks without Sage I sensed the water. It was no longer flowing, it was slowly flooding. The steady stream was in time reaching higher and the water level was rising in silence. I feared the depths and wondered if, in a moment, a tsunami would come to wash me away or – worse – it would continue to rise and insidiously drown me. All I could do was sense it rising and hope to keep my head above the water.

I felt the physical separation from Sage. My heart sought him every day. At night my spirit sat in his company. Sleep was sweet relief. In those days I stayed in the moment, leaning heavily on Spirit. In those days I took solace in not knowing or caring what would come next. I followed my nose and took one step at a time.

In honour of my parents I chose to bury Sage with a Catholic service officiated by a priest of my mother's choosing. She chose Father Mathew and I trusted her choice.

She had known and worked with him for many years. My mother had been there for each and every one of Sage's firsts and I wanted her to be with me, fully, in his last moments in earth time. My mother was to Sage, a caring Queen and his friend. My mother and Sage are more alike than Sage and I and they found deep comfort and contentment in each others company. If Sage was not with me he was with his Grandmother. Sage loved her deeply and I think sometimes preferred to be with her over me. I knew this and did not mind as one of the delights of my life was bearing witness to the beautiful relationship between my mother and my son. Fathers Day became Grandmother Day and my mother deserved it as she was Sage's secondary carer and without her I do not know if we would have been able to make it. I knew my mother's heart was breaking double-fold, she had lost her grandson and her daughter had met her worst nightmare. Loss was heavy and little comfort was available despite how much we may have tried to comfort each other. We were two broken women and I wished to lean into my mother, to invite her in.

The day before I met with Father Mathew and my mother, I sat with my sister Kath. Kath lay on my outdoor couch and watched while I played with earth and potted plants. We spoke at length about our family, our relationship to being Catholic, and the power of ritual. I asked: "What did a ceremony of Spirit and burial mean? And where was God in all that?"

As I explored my fears and hopes with Kath she listened and slowly her heat rose. By the end of the day Kath's temperature was dangerously high. A precarious place for a woman in healing post-chemotherapy. By nightfall we were in Emergency reaching for life. My sister was in distress and angry at life and death and cancer. I stayed on the sidelines and watched the nurses and doctors coming and going and held Kath's hand as she cried. My prayers for Sage merged with prayers for my sister. Kath spent three days in hospital receiving the care she needed. She was going to be okay but a long road of healing lay before her. I was aware that she and I could keep fighting. Sage's fight was over. Death had won.

THE NEXT DAY I met with Father Mathew and my mother to begin planning the burial service. We met at the church where my mother for years had been volunteering as an art teacher for those experiencing the difficulties of life with a mental illness or simply disadvantage. The church is an old and commanding space that is beautiful and cold at the same time, in the way only a church can be. Still nervous about what this meant I approached with respect. Mostly for my mother. She had lost her beloved grandson and he was to be buried with her husband. My nerves and anxiety melted as we met. Father Mathew was open and also nervous, he knew he sat in the company of pain and was obviously holding space for my mother who he had worked with for years. Father Mathew suggested we sit in a back room where we could be comfortable and I was thankful to not have to enter the church as that felt like I would be swallowed by the stained glass light and the image of Jesus on a cross. We sat at a simple table in the back room of the community space and we began tentatively. We let the nerves and intense pain spill out in a gentle way. We shared stories of God, Spirit, love, healing and song. I felt confident and comfortable to share that I wanted no talk of sin and wished for the service to be honoring of my parents and our family's foundation as Catholics. Prayers were chosen and Father Mathew suggested I write the service. He said it felt like I knew what I wanted and he was happy to follow my lead and to share my wishes. It felt like a big task to be given but I knew he was right so I asked my mother to help me.

Together, our beliefs would weave a service that mirrored the respect, faith and love our family held.

As I was leaving that day, Father Mathew stopped me at the doorway that led out to the sunshine. My mother was steps ahead and already on her way to the car. Father Mathew placed his hand on my shoulder.

"Why me? Why have you chosen me?"

I glimpsed his insecurity and felt the weight on his shoulders.

"It is not me who chose you, it was my mother. I trust her and so must you. She was clear in her choosing, you are the one she wants."

His vulnerability was evident and appreciated. In a truly human moment I saw clearly that we had all been chosen. The quote of God and trust sang in my ears and wrapped my heart. I guess God trusted us this much.

I walked away from the meeting with Father Mathew in a daze. Unsure of how the task was to be done I stayed in the moment and followed my nose. I found myself at a bar in the nearby Fortitude Valley mall. By midday on most days I reached for a drink. I could withstand the morning without screaming but only because I had promised myself a medicinal ale at midday. The liquid amber would squash the screaming and softened me into the lull I had become accustomed to. As I drank I thought of Sage. What was happening for him in his last moments? Was he aware he was leaving? Did he cry out for me? I hoped and prayed he felt no pain and sensed no fear. I wished him peace.

I stayed in the moment and continued to follow my nose

away from the bar. It led me to a musical duo playing in the busy mall. People passed and shopped around them. I felt compelled to stop. There was a lonely stool calling my name so I sat. The next song began and I found myself in awe listening to a tale of the last hour of an owl.

Fifteen Bars (by T J Quinton)

And as he reached under his left wing and handed me that slip,

I swear a shudder shook the tree

I couldn't see I said; "Is this real? Who put you up to this?"

He said "My friend you've been judged unworthy – my friend this is it."

So I put on my best Sunday suit and I, I march boldly down to hell.

I'm a liar and a thief so this says and I, I guess we all must pay our dues.

And as I waited for the guards to come, they're gonna carry me away.

Fifteen bars I was granted, as my last request, to say what I need to say.

The guards had come to take him away. To hell. It was a rainy Wednesday night in the song and on the Wednesday that Sage had passed the rain also fell. As the song continued I held the words and tune as a sign of fear being hell as they told the story of the owl and redemption. My worst fear was playing out in front of me. Was Sage met by guards? I dreamt of angels. As the set finished a connection to the musicians was made and I shared some of my story and my fear of the owl and hell. Tim, one of the musicians gifted me his CD called, Sorry Business. "Here, you need one of these," he said.

With CD in hand and my head now swimming with fears and wishes of guards and angels I journeyed to Hayley and Scott's house. Scott had spent the past week crafting an amazing gift. With his hands and talent he was building Sage's coffin. Scott is a master who works with frames for great works of art and has for years been perfecting how to turn wood into art and refreshed life. He generously offered to make Sage's coffin and I gladly received the gift Death offered. In the days before, I had wandered into my mind and asked Spirit to show me the coffin. All I was given was the image of a cardboard box. Simple. Straight lines. Each time I implored I was shown the same box.

Scott was crafting the coffin in the carport of their home. When I arrived it felt like a blaze of fire was surrounding the carport and I wondered if the fire was keeping me out or protecting the sacred space. I sat with Hayley upstairs and drank wine as a way of allowing the fire to settle. I told Hayley of the persistent cardboard box in my mind. A few glasses of wine later, I was ready to meet the coffin. My father's coffin had been handcrafted after his death in the Solomon Islands and now my son was also given this honour. I once again saw the costume and myself as the mother holding vigil.

Tentatively, I crossed the imagined fire wall and went to meet the coffin with the image of the cardboard box clear in my mind. I opened the door and saw the very same box. The cardboard was replaced with golden blonde wood, beautifully cut and polished. My heart soared. It was so beautiful. The art, the craft, the care, all so evident. My son, the master, had been gifted a coffin that matched him. Simple, with straight lines.

I stayed with Hayley and Scott, and over the next two days, an altar was built in their upstairs living room. Piece by piece we lay items at the altar to represent the passing of this time and the weight of the moment. I spent time with the coffin and felt a closeness to Sage. Prayers and wishes were sent out and the coffin was blessed. Two sage leaves were gilded and placed over the heart of the lid. Scott told stories of feeling Sage with him as he worked and I delighted in feeling that he was close. I felt immense gratitude. By the end of the two days I knew how to write the burial service. Simple, with straight lines.

On Monday, two days later, I met Scott in a park and with tears we drove to the funeral home to deliver the coffin.

One step closer. Sage would be home soon.

With a funeral service to write ahead of me, I began to seek the advice of my angels.

Angels have always grounded me. I imagine it sounds strange to others as angels are ethereal beings, not of this earth – a part of their power being ungrounded. But imagine this: an angel's love from above can keep you bound to below. Knowing and feeling them with me makes being on earth make sense.

My angels, those I seek and sense, have wings that spread wide and stretch as far as the love is needed. All I see is love and wings and they ground me. My experience of angels spreads further than above. Angels come to ground.

When Sage passed from below to above, my knowing, feeling, and loving of angels changed. I never imagined myself as one: as an angel. Being grounded was so very far from my reality when Sage left my side and passed over so simply and silently. The body of your child stops breathing and your heart breaks. The soul soars, not in joy but in connection and love. As Sage lay gone but still with me, it was his body I held, but it was his soul I sang to. I imagined him flying high, meeting souls of yesterday and forever, seeing the universe in a speck and the infinite. I sang and prayed for me, for him, and to the angels.

From the moment I came home without the body of my son I was ungrounded. By day I would float and by night I flew. I counted the minutes, hours and days waiting for him. He was gone but I felt connected. I had made sure of that; I held on tight to his spirit. He was with me – in spirit and heart. What I wanted most was to hold him. For Sage to be home and with me again.

The body of my baby came home and earth came up to meet me. I had been waiting in spirit. The day he came home my soul stood back and allowed my body to enter –

fully for the first time since his death. And my body craved him.

It felt strange to me – to feel this new feeling and the strangeness drew me closer. Three houses down, past my house on our street, you turn right. You travel three short blocks past the school and you pull into the curb, right outside the Funeral Home. I found myself the morning that Sage came home inside that home asking Dean, the Funeral Director, to guide my steps, to lead me to him. Dean had been gentle and caring as we had waited out the weeks for Sage, and with him I felt comfortable.

I confessed. "Dean, I feel strange. My body is pulling me to Sage yet I know it is only his body. His soul is with me I can feel that. Why care so much about the body when my heart and soul feel so connected?"

Dean's answer was simple. "It was a body that had come from your body. It is natural to crave him."

I made arrangements to see Sage that afternoon, to dress him for his final rest and to hold him one last time. I wanted him all to myself; to share was not an option. I wanted no-one to know. I wanted no intrusion.

I had a full day to wait out the minutes till I could be with Sage. Time to think and feel. As my body craved and yearned I felt myself float. My fantasy, imagining, and fear was that as my body met his again I would magically die to meet him in spirit. My fear crept in and knocked at my senses. Going alone seemed unsafe – I felt that I could not trust myself. My spirit stretched out and reached for him. Not to Sage but to my friend Thomas.

Thomas and I had spent time together in the weeks and months before Sage died. We spent time among trees and spoke of life and death. Thomas was studying grief and learning to be a support for people and families preparing for death. Together we spoke of his new knowings and he would share his learnings with me. In the weeks before Sage passed we spoke of how important it is for the grieving heart to be with the body and to be given time in the rituals that fold out post-death. It was because of these stories and sharing that I knew how important this time was and how it was not only important but my right. I believe angels pulled Thomas and I together and post-death Thomas became my anchor. Thomas held me as I cried. Thomas sat silently listening to my wonderings and grief. Thomas grounded me as I floated through the days after Sage passed.

It was simple. One call, little explanation. Thomas knew I was to be with the body of my son and he assured me that from a distance he would hold me to the earth. I moved forward into my fear and cravings knowing that I was safe and held.

The room was cold and clinical. I shivered as I entered alone and saw my son in his golden coffin. Sage had never looked more beautiful. He was silent and at peace. My body screamed as I held him and dressed him for bed, for the big rest, for the last time. All was still as I wept and sang to my son. I tucked him in, wrapped in his beloved godmother blanket handmade by Julie, holding his grandmother teddy, and with our favourite storybook: "I'll love you forever."

It came too soon. The moment Dean entered to tell me it was time to close the coffin and separate from Sage. I leant over a last time in an attempt to get as much of my body and heart into the coffin with Sage. Gently Dean pulled me away and together we slid the lid over and Sage disappeared under wood.

Feeling devastated but grounded I left knowing exactly where to go. I drove the short distance to the soon-to-be-filled gravesite. It felt like the only place that made sense. On the way I implored the angels to care for the body of my son. At the gravesite, I surprisingly and thankfully found my sister Sandra. Had the angels guided her there at that time so she was there to meet me? Sandra was there to prepare for the burial that would happen in two days. She was timing the travel from home to the grave to ensure we would arrive before the coffin. She was as surprised to see me as I was to see her. I told her I had just put Sage to bed for the last time. Together we cried. Together we journeyed home.

The day after I last held Sage I spoke again to Thomas. I thanked him for holding me to earth. Gently, as Thomas is, he asked me if I wished to know what he had seen. Yes! I never imagined there was more to the story. Any story that centred upon Sage had become treasure. I took a breath and waited to receive.

Thomas had been in a class, learning more about supporting people as they prepare for death. I had interrupted his day and his learning. He didn't seem to mind. He left class at the exact time I told him I would be with Sage and found a private place to sit. And from there he sat with me.

"I saw you," he said. "I saw you standing over Sage. I watched you from behind. I couldn't see your face only your back. As I watched you, watching over Sage, wings grew from your back. Big beautiful angel wings. They stretched wide and far and then folded in. Folded in over Sage."

As I heard Thomas tell me his vision, I saw it in my mind's eye. Me, Sage and the wings, stretching far, wide and folding in. For just a moment I was the grounded angel. The angels I had sung to, prayed to, implored for help – I had for a moment become one of them. For my son, or because of my son, I grew wings. In a story that tells of Sage and me, I always imagined that he would be the angel. Yet because of him, I for a moment was the angel. The grounded angel with wings far and wide enough to hold all the love and keep my heart beating on earth. Invisible to me but seen by Thomas.

ON THE DAY OF THE BURIAL, I woke screaming in tears and wanted the day to never break. The moon was now full and the final chapter of my worst nightmare had arrived. As the moon would wane again soon, so would my time with the rituals and ceremonies. The body of my child was to be sealed and buried. After this day I would never touch or see him again. With intense pulsing of pain throughout my body, I tentatively prepare for the final ritual. I cover my pain in a dark blue dress with a splash of red and see myself again as the mother holding vigil, wearing a costume. At the gravesite there are few gathered. I purposefully had invited only those close as this final ritual was intimate and about family.

The site my father had been buried in years ago was now open and deep, the ground turned over and out. The cemetery is filled with large gum trees, one close to the grave providing shade. Months before, I had come to visit my father and had noted through tears how much the tree had grown since my father had been laid to rest. I had not been to the cemetery for some time but felt compelled to visit my father, inspired by my conversations with Thomas. Was I being prepared, to see the site with fresh eyes before I was to see it again to bury my son?

The day is clear with scattered whimsical clouds. One by one I meet each gathered, to embrace them and thank them for coming. As the service starts I seat myself between my mother and my Aunt, who months before lost her beloved Barry, my uncle. Between the Elder women I feel safe. Sage is carried in his coffin by the men in my life to the grave and the service commences with simple straight lines. Mardi lights a candle to represent life, her last act as my birth partner. Julie shares the words of Mary Frye and as godmother requests us all to not cry, a request not heeded. We sing Morning Has Broken, the song sung at my father's burial, and Father Mathew leads us in prayer. At the end of the service I stand beside the grave and watch as Sage is lowered into the arms of Mother Earth. As Sage descends I let go of eleven red balloons and they float to the sky. Once released my legs buckle and I am again on the ground unable to hold myself. My Mother and Godmother Julie are by my side and hold me up and to the earth. The eleven balloons, all tied together, catch in a gum tree and I feel Sage stay a little longer. Watching over me. Gently the balloons let go and float up into the blue sky. The vigil is over and I am tired. Maybe now I can rest.

That evening I sit by the ceremonial fire pit in my garden with Godmother Julie and Mardi. Both women were with me throughout my pregnancy, and the early days with Sage in Melbourne. We three had all celebrated the birth of Sage and now sat together again, this time in the company of death and endings. We spoke very little while the fire burned as it seemed like not much needed to be said. In truth, we were all so tired. It was the end of a soul-shaking moon cycle.

Rest did not follow. The first day after the end of rituals I was restless. Godmother Julie, a heart strong and practical woman, suggested we set ourselves to a task. We turned soil and pulled up grass, we tended the earth to prepare for planting. A strip of my garden close to the back door was transformed from nothing to a flower garden. Having my hands in the earth was healing and released my moon cycle blood, my body was letting go, and new seedlings of flowers prepared to grow.

My home was filled with flowers, cards, pictures of Sage and a sense of dense loneliness. The fridge was filled with meals lovingly made by friends, mostly lasagne, one of Sage's favourite meals, which strangely kept appearing at the end of outstretched arms despite that fact that few knew of Sage's delight in lasagne. My home was full but I was not. I barely ate, drank an abundance of wine post-midday, and would walk in circles like a ghost, hoping someone would visit but also wishing to be left alone. I searched for meaning and craved being held. What needed to be done was done; what was to become of me now? And what of Sage and me? How could I stay connected to him? To continue to love him? What is a mother to do without her child?

My friend Anna had gifted me with a book – *The Tibetan Book of Living and Dying*. In it I found meaning and purpose. I was taught to share the belongings of Sage to those who needed them and to do this as a merit for his passing soul. Strongly connected to Sage, I gifted the belongings he no longer needed. Clothes and toys I could bare to part with were donated to a community center; his treasured lego robot was gifted to the Special Needs Department at his school; the books he had been given over the years were returned to the people who had gifted them and his bike found its way into the delighted hands of a boy who wanted his own bike to ride. In this way I could serve my son. The mother in me had a job.

I learned of the stages of the soul passing. According to Buddhist teachings it was to take 49 days before the soul of Sage was to leave the earth realm. I counted every day. On the 49th day I cried fresh tears and my sadness began to shift slowly to anger and a deep pain.

The 1969 Kubler-Ross model of the five stages of grief lists the first stage as denial. I'm not so sure if for me it was denial. I knew with all my being that Sage was dead and he had returned to spirit. Rather than denial there was the divine. If I allowed my spirit to seek him we could still be together. I had an open channel to the divine. My denial was to be later revealed. I now know that this model has been challenged by others, including Kubler-Ross herself, who initially developed the stages by observing the grief experience of people preparing to die, and not for those who were bereaved. The only thing that seems clear to me is that grief is not simple or straightforward, and is an invitation to divine connection.

IN MY EFFORT TO STAY CONNECTED to earth I decided I was ready to go back to work, in a small way. As a freelance consultant I had the choice of when to work and what to work on. Karen and Beth, with whom I ran a story-inspired consultancy, were keeping their hands firmly on the wheel so I felt at ease with taking a step back. One of my jobs was a direct service position at a community center. Each week I spent a day in a small office with a set budget of discretionary funds and a full list of community members in need. Their need was met with 15 – 30 minute appointments with me, where they would seek the solution to their problem. Some were immigrants who didn't understand the English instructions on complicated forms, others were people living on social security making efforts to stretch the meagre government dollars to cover all of life's needs. At least once a week I sat across from somebody who needed an emergency windfall of cash to stop their electricity from being cut off. The small budget I had each week needed to be shared among the many needs of the always full list of people seeking hope and a way out. The manager who ran the center told me clearly that there was no pressure to return to the job, and I could take as much time as I needed. I thanked her for her care but felt ready to return to the real world. I needed to feel useful again. Walking in circles around my empty home and drinking wine by the fire pit at night alone was slowly letting the waters of grief seep in. I had begun to feel sorry for myself and loathed the pity train.

My first day back I set up my small office with members' files, the cash box, and a resolve to be useful and help those in need. The first name on the list was of an indigenous woman who I had not seen before. She was in her early fifties, round in the belly and had a softness to her face despite an overall heavy feeling. She sat across from me, I smiled, and asked her how I could help. Her first words were expected,

"I am hoping for some emergency cash. I don't like asking for a hand out but I need it." I took a breath and settled in to hear more of her story. "My Uncle died."

My breath caught in my throat. Damn, what the fuck! First day back to work, first story shared, and here I am again sitting beside grief and talking of death.

"He had been living with me, so after he died it was my house that the family came to, and it was my house they stayed at for days and a few for a week or more. They all came and they all ate, and drank, and paid very little for anything. That's the way it goes with us. I gladly did it and kinda had no choice, but now I'm left with the last of the boys still staying on and growing boys are hungry often."

"I am sorry for your loss."

It felt strange being the one to say the words that had been said to me many times over in the past weeks. I turned my attention to her file to check her status and to see if she was eligible for emergency funds. I was grateful I had papers to shuffle as it gave me the chance to settle my racing mind and to work at keeping my expression neutral. As I shuffled she continued to talk about the death and what followed for her family. Something triggered me to stop my avoidance and to open to her. She obviously needed to share and I was the one sitting there, perhaps by angelic design, to receive her grief. I chose to be one of the people who would deliver the gifts that death brings. I settled back into my chair and allowed her story to fill the full alloted 30 minutes. She walked away with cash in her hand and I hoped a heart less heavy. I walked away that day happy that my heart had proved to me that, although broken, it still had room to hold space for others.

It felt like I was making my way back to 'normal' and one step at a time I would recover. The next week I returned to the small office and the list of those in need. I was on steady ground until I saw the bear. Through a window leading to a courtyard I saw the very large brown stuffed bear that for years had sat in my son's room. The gigantic bear was a gift from Mike, for Sage's first birthday, and was a stable mate in every bedroom Sage ever had. In my frenzy of letting go and gifting forward I had stuffed the bear into the back of my small hatchback and cast it out with the other donated toys and clothes. In my grief brain fog, I had not connected the dots... the donated items had ended up at this community center and were now the items out on display at the volunteer run charity stall. That damn stuffed bear broke something in me. I grabbed my phone and quickly left the center to escape and hide in the park next door. I paced and tried in vain to deepen my breath. My blood was pulsing and I was making no headway in calming myself down. In haste I pushed the buttons on my phone that would cast my lifeline. I called Godmother Julie. The sound of her voice answering my call released the river of tears and I allowed myself to float downstream. Godmother Julie always has had a way of calming me down. Weeks before Julie had offered her holiday house that was three hours drive north and empty. I had thought of the house but had no plans to go there, until that damn brown bear broke me. Running away from life, work, and chances of bears haunting me was now my desire. Plans were made for me to go to the house in a few weeks time. With a plan set I found my feet and stability again, squashed my feelings down, wiped my face, and walked back into the office with a resolve to get through the day without casting my eye upon the bear again.

NOW THAT THE DAM HAD BROKEN I was swimming in the rushing waters and working hard at keeping my head above water. On days I was not expected anywhere I would try to fill my time with walks in nature or reading or visiting someone. I wanted to be away from the house during the day as from my garden you could clearly hear the school bell ring and each chime of the familiar bells was the piercing reminder that at 3 pm I did not have to walk the short stroll to the school as Sage no longer needed me and the 3 pm bell no longer called for a hug. At night I sat by the fire and drank wine. My missing of Sage was deep and was felt in my heart space like a hammer had been banged into my chest. The garden became both my sanctuary and my prison. I had bought the house for Sage. He needed stability and we both needed to be closer to my mum and his grandmother. I felt anchored to this patch of earth but my desire to fly away grew. Staying meant walking through memories, listening for the school bell, and sitting by the fire. I had no idea where I wanted or needed to be but I knew my heart needed relief and I would not find it here. In the first year of grief, people warn you not to make any rash decisions and to make no big moves. Stay close to the ground is the warning. I was only months in and wanted to change everything and sweep away any triggers to my pain. There has always been a little bit of "fuck it" in me and it was now screaming. I knew I was caught. I was between worlds, earth and heaven, mixed in memories and grief.

ONE NIGHT I DREAMT of being in heaven. Sage was there and so were others. I was both a teacher and a student. Many lessons were being taught. I felt calm and happy. I had a sense that this was a dream space I had returned to more than once. In a new twist, my friend Thomas came to meet me in heaven. I was happy to see him and welcomed him into the circle. Without a word or warning he grabbed my hand and yanked me from heaven to earth and I landed with a thud. I woke in shock and was angry at being pulled away. I wished to stay in heaven.

That day I sought the message in the dream but it evaded me until that evening. Sitting quietly by the fire pit I heard spirit whisper,

"The healing happens on earth. You cannot stay forever in the divine. You are of the earth and that is where your lessons lie."

That is when a new pain began.

Some days as I drove my car I would fantasise of swiftly turning the wheel in front of a truck. Then I could leave earth and be with Sage. It was not that I wanted to die, I simply wanted to be with Sage. I knew I would never turn to meet the truck but my mind craved the opportunity and the twisted tale of the truck became a story my mind replayed. I kept my truck fantasy a secret as I was sure others would not understand and there was no way I wanted my mother to know.

I missed my mother and our daily routine of caring for Sage. A repeated ritual was the after work pick up at grandma's house. After the burial I found it impossible to go to the house. The pain I felt when connecting to my mother was so intense it kept me away. But it was my mother I wanted. It felt awful and so wrong that I could not see her. I knew she was in pain and I wanted to alleviate some of it but knew that was as impossible for her as it was for me. I felt like I was abandoning her.

Close to where my mum lived there is a park that overlooks a large dam of water. One day I invited my mother to meet me there. At our chosen time we both pulled up in our cars and silently walked to a picnic table and took a seat opposite each other. We found it hard to stay connected with eyes and our gaze traveled out to the water in an effort to cover up our misplaced sadness.

"I am sorry I haven't seen you so much these past weeks," I offered.

"Its ok. How are you?"

"I'm bad"

"Me too."

We each lit a cigarette and looked deeper into the water.

"I'm sorry Mum, I want to see you, to visit you at the house, but I can't. Seeing you hurts the most."

"I know."

"If he wasn't with me, he was with you." I said this aloud as a way of sharing that I acknowledged how much she would be missing him and as a way of honoring how important she was to him.

"I miss him," my mother shuddered softly.

It broke me a little. Here we were, the mother and

grandmother, tied by an unspeakable pain and unable to share it.

"He loved you so much Mum."

"I know. And I love him."

We said little else and cried sparingly. Cigarettes were extinguished and I told my mother I was planning on leaving for a while, to get some space and look to a new horizon.

"I understand," was her simple reply.

Strangely, after that day I was able to return to my mother's house. Sharing my pain out loud had taken away its power and I felt like my mother's house, despite being a site of painful memories, was again the place my mother sat and waited out the visits from her children and grand-children.

DAYS WERE PASSING and I was getting closer to my escape three hours north. One evening, three days after the 49th day, I lay in bed with pain in my belly and a burning in my Caesar scar. After all these years it felt awe-inspiring to feel my son with me again in my body. In my imaginings the umbilical cord was being cut. I howled in heart agony as I felt the separation expand and snap. I allowed myself to fall into the pain. I felt safe as in my company were a flock of angels soothing every cut and caring for me. I slept deeply that evening and woke feeling like my body had been thrashed in blows of a storm.

The next day is when anger strutted in, dressed in red and black. I had been gifted a healing treatment that was to soothe me – a detox for my pain. It did not soothe, it revealed.

I lay on a treatment table for 90 minutes and let the bottles of wine seep out of my pores. I was not relaxing into layers of release, I was slowly winding up. Following the treatment, as I walked back to my car, I sensed the shift in my energy. I was no longer stumbling. Boldly I strut forward, pounding the pavement with force. I checked into my new energy seeking the knowing of what had shifted and where I was now. Was I better? No. In my stride I found anger. There was no longer a barrier against my anger, the treatment had worn it away, and it was now out in full force. My son had been taken and those same angels who soothed me the night before were the ones who had taken him. With anger in my stride I went to war with angels.

I travelled home unsure of what anger would bring but feeling thankful that for now I felt something different. Wine was poured and I paced the back room of my house, the one that leads to the garden. I looked to the horizon and began chanting my mumbles of anger. Sip by sip the mumbles got louder and their force left my mouth as daggers.

Nina sent news from Spain and life met death again. She was pregnant with her much-wanted second child. A new child, fresh life was on the way – just not to me. My anger swelled at the angels for their cruel joke delivered now at the peak of my pain. I was happy for my friend, her wish was coming true. My wish had been stolen. Without hesitation or thought and in full force, charged with my anger, I picked up the printer from my desk and hurled it out the back door and delighted in the smashing of what was once complete but now in pieces. I took a breath and glared at the broken technology. My breath quickened and I inhaled a deep satisfaction that settled under my skin. I made a choice and this time I would not be putting myself to bed. I set to task. In the back of my car was a box filled with plates, cups and glasses that I was to take to the community centre to donate. For days as I drove they would clink and shift at each turn. Remembering them gifted me with grenades and they swiftly all followed the same fate as the printer.

With feet securely planted at the open back doorway I would raise each piece above my head and in anger let it fly to the cement. A frenzy took over and the grass, pathway and stairs of my garden filled with shatters and shards. Looking down upon them I learnt what a person who self harms may feel as the broken pieces scattered were giving me relief. I could now see outside my chest and saw my broken heart on the grass and dripping down the stairs.

Later that day, as the sun was close to setting my sister Sandra found me. I was sitting in the garden, at a distance under the Jacaranda tree, looking through anger upon the broken pieces. She stood at the top of the stairs and took in the mess. Carefully she navigated her way through the war zone avoiding possible land mines. The close sight of her softened me and my truth surrendered.

"They took my baby away," I whimpered.

"Who, Deb?"

"The angels. They took my baby away."

Gently my sister took me inside and sat with me while I oscillated between agony and anger. I was so angry at my angels. What gave them the right to take my baby? He was mine. I had made him, and I was caring for him. It was irrational but to me very real. Anger felt good and I fed it.

The next day I put my house on the market. Sandra arranged for her real estate agent to visit and he appraised my house, broken pieces and all. He professionally ignored the war zone and pointed out the features that would make my home a good sell. He was good at spinning the story, the gift of a true salesman, so I bet on him. I was clear with intent and asked him to get me a quick sale so I could be set free.

For five days I smashed anything that would break. It felt satisfying to see the mess grow. Finally, the outside world looked like I felt inside. Noone dared to stop me and the war raged. As the days passed my anger slowly softened and a deep disturbance settled. "They took my baby away" became my mantra. Feeling intense anger at angels was the seed of my disturbance. My heart knew that they did not wish me the pain and it was not by their demand, but my anger needed to place blame. For years I had looked to angels for healing and guidance and now they were dressed in my anger as thieves and enemies. Part of the pain was my missing of them. Who could I pray to now?

I committed to the anger. If this was where I was then I felt obliged to travel through in the hope that if I allowed its fullness to be revealed and expressed maybe it would pass. I remembered that my loss had lessened when I had invited others to join me so I sent out word again. I invited family and friends to a smashing party. I did not want to hide my anger and felt that others may wish to also express and smash. On the evening of the fifth day of smashing, people arrived to the smashing party. The invitation was to come armed with something to smash, to drink wine, and eat smashed pumpkin soup. I was at the end of my anger and felt one last push towards letting it go. Those who came took their turn in smashing something and letting it go. I stood with them all as they declared what their anger was directed at and then with a howl or a squeal their smash joined the war. I drank wine and the frenzy whirled up again. As I smashed I felt the need for more, the satisfaction was waning and I wanted a hit of the feeling that for five days had held me. My last memory of that night is dragging the small purple bookshelf out of Sages room and hurling it down the stairs. In my drunken haze I wanted it to smash into smaller pieces so I stumbled into the broken pieces to retrieve the shrapnel of shattered wood. My friends Richard and Justine pulled me out of the mess and ended the war. Soon after I was put to bed.

Upon waking I felt raw and disgusted. I was amazed that I had no cuts after my stumble into the mess. The anger had made me very tired. Looking upon the brokenness now left me with pain. The pleasure was gone. I knew for certain that I was prepared to make a mess but not to clean it up. I hired a man and his two young apprentices to clean up and remove the evidence. Sitting with my hangover and resolve to surrender, the man approached me.

"This is a bigger job than I had thought."

"Yeah, so?" I was in no mood for games.

"Well I quoted you a $100 but....." To me he looked as smashed and ugly as my garden.

"$100 is all I have. Take it or leave." Anger is truly ugly and I had no care or kindness in me.

"Will you pay me in cash?"

"Does this look to you like a job I need a receipt for?"

He nodded and the three of them pulled on thick gloves and began the work of clearing and removing all evidence of anger, war, and my broken heart. I hid in my bedroom and cried.

Later that day I drove away. It was time to talk to the angels. Months later Nina's second son was born, my third godson. On the day he was born, my heart swelled and I felt my capacity for love deepen.

On the odd night when I am drifting to sleep I see myself drawing back a wine bottle or glass in the way an archer would pull on the bow, and my mind sets it free. When I see this image flash and feel the smash, I know my almost sleeping self is letting me know that anger is in me somewhere and is seeking a release.

I TOOK WITH ME books, journals, music and good food. I left behind the alcohol and cigarettes. It was time to become clear. I needed clarity to listen. I had many questions for the angels and I wished desperately to hear their reply. I journeyed to Poona, a small fishing town three hours north from home. Pulling in to Poona felt like I had arrived in the ghost town of a B grade TV movie. It was very quiet on the streets and there was little movement between the houses and the shore. The house I was gifted by Julie and her family was a typical small house that is a home to no-one and everyone. The curtains were thick and dark and did not match the cushions or the couch. The walls were lined with the odd picture frame that looked like the choice had been made to not remove the 'in place for sale only' images. I settled in for the night as the sun was setting and wondered for more than a moment: what the fuck am I doing here? I had arrived at a new chapter and had no idea of how it was going to play out.

The first morning I ventured out to seek the water. Down by the sea, I saw a family of pelicans. My Dad loved pelicans. When we were all younger my father set to task and over many months, extending into years, he built a holiday home by a river. Many weekends as a child we would drive to Alexandria to our plot of land by the river and play the days away as dad and my brother built our holiday home. Once close to completion, my dad declared that the home was to be named Pelican Walk, as he loved to watch the sunset, and the pelicans at the river after a day's building. After his passing, the sight of them reminded me of him. The pelicans assured me that my father was in attendance. At least I know one person here, I thought. Each morning I would meditate, journal and run. Towards or away I was still unsure.

I reached out to heaven with my questions. It took three days before I heard any answers.

Death is not the ending. It is a transition. Love and peace are possible. Love never dies.

That was soothing but not enough for me. I needed them to answer my questions. Why had they taken my baby away? Why was I not warned? As I softened into the silence over the days the angels stroked my heart and whispered the answers I sought.

One morning I ran to exhaustion and fell upon the grass under a tree that borders the sand. Without thought and with my focus on breathing deep into my lungs I heard the message I had been chasing for days.

"*Nothing went wrong that day,*" they told me. "*Sage was always going to leave. Both Sage and I knew that. We had not only been warned, we had planned it. My teacher Sage had left me to deepen the lessons of love. Sage's work was now in heaven and mine was on earth.*"

And then my father whispered, "*I am here too, loving you.*"

Over the next few days I was counselled to continue to love Sage and to learn to love without attachment, anger or fear. A gift I have received is my opening again to listening. I desperately wanted to be connected to Sage and to hear what the angels had to say. In my opening to hear Sage and the angels, I opened to hearing Spirit and my inner voice of intuition, the voice of my higher self. Over the years I had learnt to dampen that voice, I had edited my listening. I would choose to turn up the volume when it suited me or was needed. But I also chose when to turn the volume down. Sage's death re-connected me to a steady stream of guidance. While I was reconnecting and learning to trust my listening again, I would ask for reassurance. As I became clear and listened I learned to ask for clarity. Send me a "without a doubt" sign I would ask. The signs always arrived. A song, a feather, dandelion flowers, red balloons, and pictures or quotes from famous inventors. Bit by bit, sign by sign, I released the barriers I had built that kept the flow of the divine at bay.

I felt a call to action. My ticket to heaven could not be cashed in until my work on earth was done. I vowed to not live a little life. I was unsure of what I was meant to do but sure that there was more to come. Possibilities swam in my head and I remembered the many other people living lives through the best and the worst. I reinforced my promises to myself and I began to let go of attachment, anger and fear.

For days I allowed the pain to howl and my heart to crush. I began to take notes as messages came through. Toward the end of my retreat I would wake and ask if I could go home that day. *"No,"* I was told. *"More is needed"*. I continued to write, run, meditate and listen. On the 12th day I was told I could go. I was advised to clear Sage's room and to prepare myself to journey. I was directed to write – I was not sure what, but the message was clear – write. It was time to let go and to transform.

Reconnected to Sage, my father, and the angels, I drove away from Poona just as the sun began to melt into the horizon. The long stretch of road was empty and the drive felt easy as I hugged the mountain that shouldered the road. I curled around a bend and was met by the sharp lights of a truck. Shocked I swerved, which turned my car towards the mountain. I swerved again to avoid hard destructive rock. I was now beyond the central line and in front of the truck. One last swerve saved my life as I screeched past the truck, screaming with my hand on the horn. Moments later, further down the mountain road, after my breath calmed, I realised I had met the truck I had been dreaming of. Rather than allowing it to crush me I chose to save my own life. I was earthbound and alive.

SAGE'S FAVOURITE SONG was *The Sum of it all* by an Australian band, The Herd. If it played in the car he would jig along and sing to the tune. It was the only song he seemed to notice. I asked him one day what he liked about it and in true Sage style he replied, "I don't know, I just like it." After Sage passed this song found me and followed me. In my search for meaning I attempted to glean a deeper message. Finally one day I released and listened, not to the lyrics, but to what Sage had told me. Sometimes we don't need to know, we just need to like it.

The Sum of it all by The Herd

Opening lyrics:

What is the trade off in your life? What did you pay? What is the price?

What did you weigh it up against? Was it worth it?

ONCE HOME, I followed the advice I was given and began by dismantling Sage's room. I asked my mother to help and together we cried as the sum of it all, Sage, and his ten years was packed away. Over the next weeks I dismantled my home and with Sandra's help dressed it up for sale. Pieces of my life were sold, treasured items were boxed, and anything that equaled Deb and Sage was removed. I was not sure yet where I was going but it was time to go. My home slowly transformed from the home Sage and I had shared into a house that looked nothing like us. In those days I felt like I was slowly dying. Sage had been given the quick death and mine was slow. As I walked about the house that was once my home I felt like a ghost. Haunting the past. Stuck in the present. Alive and dead with nowhere to go.

My missing of Sage deepened and pain was an everyday enemy sitting in my chest. Most nights I sat by the fire pit and wished the days away. Winter was upon me and I waited for the lengthening of the day and for spring. I felt assured that in the spring I would come back to life. I bargained with Spirit and promised to stay in the centre of grief if they would move me swiftly through the pain. At the time I believed it to be a fair deal. At the time I believed anything that gave me some relief.

I continued to seek the centre and kept a steady gaze forward. I reminded myself that nothing had gone wrong that day. That my son was happy and free. That all was as it was meant to be. But I missed him. I missed my friend. I wondered about me. What was next? I was aware I was moving through but again had no idea where I was headed.

One day at home, out at the flower bed Julie and I had built the day after the burial, I was lost in my missing of Sage. My mind was on repeat telling me over and over that I missed him, as if in a moment I may forget and need to be reminded. As my mind chanted "I miss you" my shoulders rolled in and my heart centre would collapse. While focused on a fresh bloom in the bed I reflected. It is only possible to miss someone this much if you had loved them this much. So I wondered what would happen if I chose to focus on the love, rather than the missing. Each time my mind would begin the tired chant of missing I changed the words. "I love you. I love you. I love you." My shoulders stretched out wide and my heart space opened. I had a choice, and I was choosing love, one chant at a time.

Love was evident. Those who had gathered in my garden, those present at the ceremonies' and those who also missed Sage, took great care to care for me. I felt held by prayers, wishes and kindness. At the time I was aware of those with me and I was aware that without them I would fall and may never get back up.

During the winter I was gifted with escape routes. Generous friends gifted me with tickets to fly away. And I did. I went South, North and across the sea. I began to glimpse what was possible beyond my garden. I had choices and had been gifted freedom. I was mostly grateful to be moved away, to be forced out of my garden where the school bell from Sage's school could still be heard.

Each time I left, it hurt. Each time I flew back, it hurt. There seemed to be no place that didn't hurt, but being away felt better somehow. When I left it felt like I was leaving Sage and when I returned it was fresh again ... I am going home and my baby is not with me. The wheels of a plane hitting the tarmac on a return flight to Brisbane was especially painful. The times away over the winter gifted me with seeds of new knowing, space for reflection, and times to laugh and dance. I still cried but it was balanced by life-affirming moments of possibility. The world outside my garden grew.

My trip North was gifted by my friend Brains (known to some as Sheree, but to me she is Brains). I flew to the North end of Australia and from there we ventured further into the bushland at Litchfield National Park. With our back-packs filled with supplies needed for a three-day camp we walked the worn path of divided thick bushland for almost an hour, to arrive at an isolated campsite at Walker Creek. There, in our makeshift camp, we played in three bodies of water over three days. We decided one was the past, one the present, and upstream was our potential future. Together we explored choice and possibility. I allowed the past to seep into the water and be washed away. I chose carefully in the present what I was to keep in my heart and in the future a steady wash of water fell. I was again at a place where the water flows.

Over the three days I was able to sit high and gain a new perspective. Close and just across from the water that represented to us the present, was a stone hill that was not easy but possible to climb. As the sun was ready to set each afternoon we would take our day and a cup of wine up the hill to watch the glory of light in 360 degree goodness of gold and color. The water, the height, the open sky, all revealed the image of myself grabbing at straws in the hope one was my future. I reminded myself that patience is needed and running toward a new life simply to have one was not the promise I had made for myself. I released further into letting go and allowing the time it takes to grieve. I wished the best for myself. I chose to change from the known place of being led by my mind and to trust my heart as the leader. I chose to feel more and think less. I released into letting go so my heart could show me the next stone to be laid on the path.

DEEPER INTO THE WINTER I flew across the sea to Indonesia. A serendipitous return. One year before I had been there. Sage was home and I was away. I had traveled to Indonesia for a work conference and had planned days away after working for myself to simply be, have a holiday, enjoy myself. Respite from the suburbs and life as a single mother. What I found was sadness. I did not want to be there alone. I missed Sage and my garden. I cried for two days and finally surrendered. I flew home early with a renewed commitment to Sage and our life. The day I flew home I wanted to run to the school and release Sage early so I could receive the big squeezy hug I craved. Knowing that Sage did not like surprises or unexpected changes of plan I waited to hear the school bell. Sage, expecting his Grandmother, ran into an excited embrace that I collapsed into. While walking towards home I told him I had wanted to come early, before the school bell.

"Yeah well mum, it is good that you didn't. That would be breaking the rules."

I smiled and my heart skipped at how nuanced and quirky my little old man was. In the months that followed Sage and I grew from strength to strength. I softened as a mother and together we laughed more. I practised patience while listening to the lengthy explanations of Sage's inventions and began to get comfortable with our rhythm.

On the 100th day since Sage had passed and one year to the day of my last trip I was again in Indonesia. I was with friends on a small island, Gili Meno. I awoke the morning of the 100th day to the early call to prayer from a nearby mosque. It was still dark and everyone was sleeping. As the sky lightened in response to the rising sun I pondered what to feel. 101 days ago I did not know that my life would be forever changed. I did not know that I would be on a beautiful island in Indonesia. Half awake and half in a dream, I saw an image of myself standing at the shore. I picked up my heavy grief and I tossed it into the sea. *"It doesn't have to be heavy,"* I heard. *"You can let go and still love."* I got out of bed and walked to the water.

That morning I walked the shore of the island with my friend Justine. It took me some time before I could share what this day was and meant. In true Juz style she listened and let it all be. As the day carried on I shared more with Juz and others. That night I danced and celebrated making it to the 100th day. Those with me hugged me and wished me well. I smiled and laughed. And the whole time I was falling in love with Sage all over again. Any moment I felt guilt over dancing and laughing I felt Sage. I felt my son gently pushing me to open further to love and to my future.

While in Indonesia, I chose the first step and stone on the path to my future. I chose to return to Sri Lanka, the other island that had opened my heart a year earlier. In January 2012, I left Sage in the safe and loving care of my mother. I travelled to Sri Lanka to work on Theatre of Friendship, a community theatre project that builds friendships to build peace.

In the first workshop I facilitated with one of the Sri Lankan theatre groups, when they learned I was a mother, I was asked by one of the men why I had left my son.

"In my culture the mother does not leave the child. Why are you here?"

It was a genuine question of curiosity. While responding I melted and told the truth. I was missing Sage. It was a sacrifice to be here with them and not with my son but I wanted to share my gifts with them and the world. I ended by telling the group that if I needed to hug them too much that was simply the mother in me.

Melting and crying in front of a group was not my standard response. My past action would have been to get harder not softer. Maybe it was the heat in the theatre that day that melted me, maybe I was ready and willing to be vulnerable. As I deepened into my work in Sri Lanka I became known as 'mumma'. To them, I was their mother.

It was the mother in me that wanted to return to Sri Lanka. But first I needed to live out the winter and watch as my old life slowly dismantled. During the winter and into the early days of spring I fell often back into the fire. I would try too hard and forget to allow. I would be led by thoughts and not feelings and most days I cried. In moments I would allow and be guided by feelings. I was learning.

A DAY JUST SHY OF SPRING, I lay under a tree at the university I had attended years before with Nick. I was assisting my brother-in-law with a workshop he was teaching. The day was warm and beautiful. The tree was outside one of the classrooms I had spent many hours in, many years before, and I pondered the cycles and rhythms of life as I gazed up into the wide and full green light the tree was filtering. On this day under the tree my whole self relaxed – for just a moment, I let go.

In a swift shift an image rose from my feet and flew up my right side and landed confronting and menacing at my face. I was well tuned to this image as it was the moment my heart shattered and heaven broke open. The day I went to wake Sage, to find that his spirit had flown in the night, that his heart had stopped, and that he had let go.

My haunting began the days that followed after the incident under the tree. Catching me unawares at random moments the image would sweep up to scare me and each time it grew in strength. I refused to be haunted. I wished for magic and was not prepared to live out my days fearing the taunting image.

I sought help and said yes to the counselling appointment that my doctor had set up for me weeks before. I walked into the small couch-centered room ready to tackle and take down the haunting. I met with a young counsellor, fresh faced with wide eyes. I shared with her my story and immediate need to exorcise the energy that allowed the image to scare me. I watched her face try hard at maintaining neutral. I say trying as she was not doing a good job. I left unsure of what had transpired on the couch but knowing it was not only myself that was feeling uncomfortable. Two days later I received a call from my new therapist awkwardly explaining that after my appointment she had spoken to her supervisor and they had both agreed that she was too young to take on my story. I knew it was the right choice but could not help feeling like I had been dropped like a hot potato. I was recommended two other therapists and after calls with them received the same response.

"Sorry, I can't help you."

'Seriously, what the fuck?' was my overarching thought. Was I not the therapist's dream? A patient who knew exactly what they needed. All I was missing was the one who would guide me to the transformation I was seeking. One afternoon with this mission in sight I began googling. I was determined to find someone who would say yes to me. Several calls later and feeling more than just a little rejected I finally reached someone who spent enough time to understand my request.

"Oh, I see. What you need is different. You are not seeking a counsellor. You need a psychoanalyst or maybe someone who works in hypnotherapy."

I focused my google search and typed in psychoanalyst and hypnotherapy. Top of the search was Dr John and one phone call later my first appointment was made. Dr John advised me that I may not get to what I was reaching for but he assured me he would be with me as navigator on the journey.

Gently, through hypnosis, Dr John and I shifted the

image. I was asked to give Sage words for the haunting image. My intuition told me the words were, "Goodbye Mum." Over time and in process the image weighted with the words of Sage, shifted from one that swept up close to scare and taunt, to the image of me standing on the edge of a cliff, arms open, looking out over the world. In this image Sage was in spirit behind me and beaming love through my back heart chakra space. In this image my spirit stretched wide. I felt calm and grounded. I let go. From this place Sage whispered:

"All the love you have for me give it to the world."

I left the session with a fresh vision and renewed hope. The haunting was over and Sage in spirit had given me direction. Another layer of letting go was needed. I further released my attachment to Sage and fell further into love. Sage's task of being with me in earth time was done and to love him meant letting his spirit release further from the earth where I would ask him to sit. I needed to let him fly. Letting go has never been easy for me. My resistance had strengthened my resolve to hold on over the years. And now I was being asked to let go. It was the scariest thing to do but seemed to be the best possible course of action. It was my third wish for myself in action. I found it difficult to let go for me, but for Sage I would do anything. To love him was to let him go. I leant into another layer of surrender and I let go. I journeyed out into the world to give my love away.

A new message from Sage emerged: *"Just go mum!"*

I CRIED SAYING GOODBYE to my beloved Jacaranda tree and it was bittersweet to walk away from the home I had built with Sage. Hayley and Scott hosted a final dinner at their home. Once again Hayley and I built an altar. This time the magic woven was not of endings but transitions. At the altar I saw our next project. Hayley and I were to work with children and their dreams. It involved a book, *Imagine a Day*. A book Hayley had gifted Sage when he was six, but was now at the altar as it had been re-gifted back to Hayley when all Sage's books were released. In a spark the project ignited. I flew away the next day full of hope and a belief in impossible dreams.

"Imagine a day when the ordinary becomes the extraordinary. A day when anything is possible."

Once on land in Sri Lanka I felt myself slowly falling through layers. As is the usual rhythm in Sri Lanka, things were busy. There are no straight lines and everything seems to take much longer than you think it is going to. The air is thick with humidity and the smells of cooking oil, coconuts, and curry. I reconnected to my friends and colleagues who share the Theatre of Friendship project. It was like a release into a new vibration. For weeks I had been watching as my old life slowly dismantled. Piece by piece it was packed away, sold, broken, or buried. The vibration was a painful dance in slow motion. And now I was here, useful again, moving to a new and improved beat, among the people who had been at a distance, holding light for me.

Returning to Sri Lanka was going to the place where many called me mumma. My heart stitched up a little each time I heard them call me by my Sri Lankan name. They allowed me to mother them and to be their friend. I gratefully accepted, but wondered, "Where is Sage in this landscape? Has he come with me across the sea or is he now further into the sky?"

In the opening ceremony of our time together Father Ron, a leader in the project, shared a meditation with us all in the circle. There were fifty of us, some very well-known to me, some new to the group. We were together to share theatre, stories, friendship and the hope of peace. I wished peace for them and I wished it for myself. As the meditation was closing and Father Ron was speaking the final words a beautiful voice began to sing. For a moment I thought maybe it was an angel.

"We will overcome. We will overcome. We will overcome this."

Others began to sing. We sang to share and to be together. To acknowledge the peace that we all sought. I allowed myself to cry. To release into the song and to take this moment of being with them all in this circle, all seeking peace. I was unsure of how long it would take for peace to find its way into my heart that was broken and bruised after the last months of watching my old life die. My heart was open, bleeding, and being held by shaking hands.

The angel singing was Father Tony. He was new to me and to most others in the circle but he had silently been with us before. He moved gracefully with an open heart and a beaming smile. He held enough space for others to be seen and to feel warm. I believe him to be an earth angel.

That evening word came from Australia. My sister Sandra sent word that the deal was done and my house was under contract. The next day she sent word again. Overnight the Queen had fallen, the Jacaranda tree was now in pieces. There had been no storm, lightning or strong winds. There is no rhyme or reason why. The Queen had split at the center of her throne. She split and fell over the neighbouring gardens. Lying broken, her branches felt the true gravity and weight of her old and well-worn wisdom.

I did not cry the day when Sandra called to share with me that the house was under contract to be sold. I did cry, and howl, the next day when she told me the tree was dead. The Queen had fallen as Sage had. We had all left the home and garden.

It took me days but I eventually heard my Queen again: "Get off." I remembered her warning wood tone. It was not a push away, it was a safety call. She knew she was old and weak and knew she could sit with me, but not hold me. Fresh grief lay open. All that had been my home was dead, broken or gone. And here I was, slowly falling through layers. There was no going back now.

Over our days together we worked and shared stories through theatre. On the third day Father Tony heard the story of Sage's passing. He opened to me and together we navigated the story and my broken heart. Father Tony had also lost loved ones and was healing from grief. The year before three members of his family had died. Father Tony spoke openly about his initial anger at God and how he sought peace. To hear a priest openly talk of anger at God gave me permission to realise that my anger ran deeper than angels. I needed a conversation with God. I asked Father Tony if I could attend mass with him the next morning. He offered to hold a service for Sage and me.

That night while wrapping up work I realised that all day my left ear had been bothering me with a subtle burning feeling. I pulled on it and remarked to my friend Anna that something strange was pulling at my left ear.

The next morning I woke early to attend mass. My friend Alex came with me and we sat in silence in the small and beautiful chapel. Hymns were sung in Tamil and Father Tony summarised the service in English. Raised a Catholic, I was able to follow despite the language barrier. Prayer is prayer. I spent the service opening to my conversation with God. I was pissed at God but knew to stay in the centre of the prayer to seek connection there. I missed Sage. Why couldn't God give him back? Here I was again at bargaining. The final prayer was announced. I closed my eyes and stayed with my plea. "Please God, give me my son back." I committed to staying in the centre of the prayer. It hurt but I stayed with my eyes shut tight. The seal broke and Sage came through.

"I am your left ear. I am always by your side"

I dissolved in pain and gratitude. This was the best God could do. My son was with me in spirit. I opened my eyes to an empty chapel. Everyone had left. It was just me, Sage and God. I slowly approached the altar and released an animal howl of pain. God and I have more conversations to come but for now Sage was with me. Had God given me this or was it my allowing?

FOR WEEKS I TRAVELLED around Sri Lanka teaching and volunteering my skills. I met with war widows, children who had lost parents, young people wishing for a new future and adults ready to stand as change-makers.

My first journey took me north, to Jaffna and Kilinochchi, the heartland of the recent civil war. I stayed for weeks with Rev. Phillip and his team of artists and changemakers working to rebuild lives. My first task was to teach English to a group of preschool teachers. I felt very under-qualified and nervous. On my first day I was met by twenty women with beaming open smiles. I had never taught English before, they had never been taught by a foreigner. We were all a little lost. The women are given little opportunity for training and development and they all opened to the task of learning and committed to doing their best. I felt like I had to meet them there, but my truth was I felt lost and tired. I spent the day in the heat teaching songs and phrases. It was not my finest hours as a teacher. I was trying so hard to hide my truth that I exhausted myself. That night as I lay awake I realised that in my trying so hard I had spent an entire day with twenty fascinating and committed women and I knew next to nothing about them and they knew very little about me. My exhausted soul beckoned me to relax my heart and open to the women.

On the second day of teaching I announced that the morning session was to be dedicated to us as wonderful women and together through broken English and learning, we would share stories. I started by teaching them the song Beth had played at Sage's memorial; *The river is flowing.*

We spent time learning the words and the rhythm and together we sang. Together standing in a circle, I shared the story of the song and its importance to me. Hiruni, a mother herself and one of the teachers, reached out and grabbed my arm. I was not sure if she was holding me or holding on to hold herself up. Hiruni has two children. Her husband was held by the post-war government in prison for many years. She knows loss and she stood with the hope she would see him again and her children would know their father. She had hope and mine was gone, my chat with God had assured me that no matter how much I begged I was not getting my son back. I looked around the circle of women and saw them seeing me. I was now visible and vulnerable and it felt supportive. With hearts open we began to share stories. Each woman spoke as much as she could in English, for some a daunting task. We laughed, shared and listened. One by one we all became visible.

At the end of my time with the women we held a graduation ceremony. As a surprise, the women, all holding tight to their deserved graduation certificates, spontaneously erupted into singing *The river is flowing* as a gift of appreciation to me as their teacher. I was so proud of them all. That day I reflected: if I help the women, they will help the children. A grateful task for the mother without a child.

After the women, I met the children. Rev Phillip asked me to run happiness workshops for some children in a special program. I was unsure what a happiness workshop was so I questioned further. In North Sri Lanka many children have lost one or both of their parents due to years of civil war. They have suffered trauma and loss. Happiness workshops are the antidote. Now I had truly met my match. I had lost the child, they had lost the parent. Together we made two halves to a whole.

I was unsure of what I would see or feel when I met the children. Would they be sad or scared? Could I make them happy, even for a short time? Thankfully the universe had provided me with my own playmates: Samadhi and Aaron. I met Samadhi before going North. She was in Sri Lanka doing research for her PhD and her partner Aaron was visiting. They turned up just in time for the happiness workshops. And happiness is what we found. The children were delighted to see us and so eager to play. Through laughter and silliness I was able to forget that we had all lost love. The children were saying yes to life and showing me that I could do so if I wanted to. "Play some more," they would invite. And when they hugged you they meant it. I smiled a lot in the days of the happiness workshops.

All around me were people amidst post-war devastation getting on with rebuilding their lives and their homes. It was while I was up North that my house settlement in Brisbane was finalised. I felt the irony when invited the next day to the blessing ceremony for a family's new home they had built with the help of aid funding. The family was settled and happy, after a long time waiting, they now had a cement home to replace their temporary tent housing. They invited me to plant the palm tree in the front garden that to them was the augur of good fortune. Inside the home, a woman from a nearby village, known as the fire woman, lit the first fire in the hearth at the center of the home. Ceremonial rice milk was shared with those in attendance. I was so happy for the family, and so aware that I now had no home, not even a tent.

Over the next few weeks I continued to travel the island and to teach. Most days I taught storytelling theatre to creative and engaged groups of grateful students. My teaching revealed a repeated message. "Don't rush, allow the scene to naturally evolve. The story will come one scene and moment at a time." Through a few towns I travelled with Amila, a young musician and theatre maker, who used his English skills to take on the task as my translator. A late and hot afternoon we sat in the shade drinking a cold beer. I shared a few details of my fear of what now, and where would I go after my time in Sri Lanka. He sipped the beer and grinned. As my translator he had translated my teaching through three towns and many workshops and knew me well. Amila reflected back to me. "Slow down Mumma. Don't rush. Let it naturally evolve."

Good advice for a woman hell bent on making the death of her son mean something. For a woman desperately searching for a new life. For a woman who believed that you could bargain your way through the centre of grief.

AFTER WEEKS OF TEACHING it was time to be silent again. The travel and the teaching kept me busy and full. It was time to empty. To be silent. Two of my Sri Lankan friends took me to a Buddhist meditation retreat and introduced me to a highly respected monk, Venerable Lakshani. I retreated for a week under his guidance.

The first night of my retreat the sky darkened and a fierce thunderstorm raged. The electricity was cut and I was alone in my small cottage in the dark. The storm was so loud. It felt like it could possibly crash through the tin ceiling. Alone in the dark, deep grief found me. After weeks of trying to outrun grief I was caught in the storm. I released into a scream. No one could hear me as the thunder cascaded overhead. I cried and screamed myself to sleep. The pain was deep and thankful to be released. I had been holding on for too long.

Each morning I was granted time with Venerable Lakshani for teaching and guidance. I was told the day before by a novice monk what time I was to go to the main house. At my allocated time I would go and sit on the veranda at a distance and in the company of Venerable Lakshani and a young monk who could speak english. Venerable Lakshani is old, but it is not just his body that tells the tale of years past, it is in his everything, the way his bones move, in how despite slight limbs sits comfortably on the floor, and his soul is seen through his wide grin and enquiring soft eyes. You get the sense that he knows much more than he is willing to say, as he also knows only a few would fully understand the depth of his knowledge. For the first two days in attendance I cried. My soul had been slowly catching the drips of my grief that was now overflowing. For two days, Venerable Lakshani watched me cry. He told me through translation that it is natural for the mother to cry. He spent our first two days together telling me stories of mothers that the Buddhist scriptures share and simple meditation instruction. I cried and listened. Once my allocated time was up he would grin, giggle a little at me, and then tell me to go meditate.

I learned that grief would always find me. There was no use in hiding or running as she would find me. And yes she wears black, with wings wide and strong enough to hold your heart.

On the third day sitting in his company I did not cry. Venerable Lakshani told me that now the work could begin. He asked me if I believed in life after death and reincarnation. I replied yes.

He nodded and began, "Good. Then you know that you have cried for this boy before and you will cry again. So when you cry, allow, but then pass on. For you will cry for this boy again." Something in that spoke directly to my heart. My tears still fell but I allowed them to pass. I found silence and sat with Grief. She invited me in. She was dressed in her standard black, I wore white.

Towards the end of my stay I shared with Venerable Lakshani that I was able to share and help others and found that easy. But what of me? How was I to manage the steady flow of pain that collected and released the drips of my grief?

"The love you have for your son you must now give not only to others but also to yourself," he told me.

Damn. The deeper lesson in love. It is much easier to love others. Now I needed to learn to love me. Damn. I knew this was the key to the lock but I also knew this lesson would take time and care. Loving others seemed easy compared to the weight I felt in loving myself. I left knowing that I would one day return. I wished to give a gift to Venerable Lakshani before I left but was told, despite being given many gifts, he did not expect them and it was best for me to simply say thank you. I realised the greatest gift I could give him was to follow his guidance and learn new edges of love and peace. Many lessons were awaiting me, but first I needed to practise what I had been taught.

I MISSED MY FAMILY. The straws had been drawn and the dominos continued to fall. We were all being shifted and challenged. The healing crisis was upon us. I felt a pull home. Soon but not yet. In my last week I was granted a reprieve. Hayley arrived and our project, Imagine a Day was birthed.

Learning to love myself was pushed to the back of the line as I dreamt up and created possibilities of the project with Hayley and the young men of Embilipitiya Black Box Theatre. Loving Sage and honouring his memory was easier so I followed the path of least resistance. Learning to love myself would have to wait. I convinced myself that I would get there in time but the time was not now. There was too much to be done and my family needed me. It was time to go home.

For weeks I had craved my family. It had been difficult to hear of their struggles and healing from afar. And for weeks I had desired to visit Sage's grave. Seeing my family and visiting Sage satisfied my needs. And then what? I was back in Brisbane. The place I had left behind and here I was again. Back home with no home to go to. For what? For only a short time I assured myself.

Scared at the depth of feeling possible back home in Australia I crowded my life with friends, parties, movement between cities and rivers of wine. I raced from one event to the next, hoping that I could outrun pain and drink away reality. At the time it was easy to do. It was summer and everyone was celebrating. I fed the celebration and movement and denied my need to be still and cry.

Christmas came like rolling thunder that threatens a storm. The Driscoll family gathered again in the Blue Mountains days before Christmas to be together. Were we celebrating? Each of us had been shifted, torn and challenged, and we gathered wearing our wounds. The Driscolls are a strong clan. For the children of the family we smiled and created spaces for love. I missed Sage deeply. He had loved Christmas and delighted in the magic of it all. Until his death, Sage believed in the fullness of Christmas magic. I was sure that one December soon he would learn the truth of the tale and see the Christmas ruse for what it was. His last Christmas Sage said to me:

"Mum, I know the Santa in the shopping mall is not real."

Ah, here it is, the moment that the child's belief in the North Pole, reindeer and elves shatters.

"Yes Sage," I simply replied.

"I know that is just a man in a costume. Santa is too busy with the elves and getting ready to turn up everyday to the shops. But don't worry, I won't tell anyone."

The magic of Christmas was intact and the story was maintained. I loved him for his belief in magic.

In the mountains, without Sage and magic, I craved to fall away, to creep into denial and to cease feeling. I wasn't sure how to be. I was lost within my own family. Feeling stuck in the torture of a Christmas without Sage I surrendered. The winter before, Kath and her family had planted a tree for Sage. With my sister Jude and niece Tara we decorated the tree. With tinsel and a star Sage arrived at

175

Christmas. My heart relaxed a little. I was relieved he was in our company.

My heart was still twisted by an unknown fear. I walked one day around the lake near my sister's home seeking to meet the fear. I walked for some time before my heart gently told me my fear was that one day Sage and his memory would not be in our company. That his memory would soften over time and he would be forgotten. I feared that the children in our family would grow and the stories would shift and change so far away from the early days of being with and without Sage.

I needed a response to my fear so I bought a ceremonial candle and gifted it to my mother at our Christmas feast. The candle represents everyone in our clan who can't be with us as each year winds down to Christmas. I gifted it to my mother, as, where she is, Christmas is.

The next day most of us left the mountains. I felt further relief. I assured myself that it would be some time before I returned to where Sage had last been. I imagined that it may even be years. My mind needed to tell me this tale so my heart would relax. Spirit had other ideas but I was not to know yet.

Over the New Year I camped, danced and drank with many fabulous friends at the Woodford Folk Festival. This dark year was finally coming to a close and I wished to dance it away. I was tired from running but determined to dance. My sister Heather and I left early to set up camp. We set the scene and waited for our playmates to arrive. In twos, threes, and fours the playmates landed at camp. Each day I called "dance of the day" and we would gather at a stage to dance our cares and worries away.

On site at the festival, a labyrinth devoted to love and partnership was built. I attended the opening ceremony and was asked by the ritual to place my intention for love. In that moment it was clear. I would devote my love to learn more about loving beyond the body and earth time, to continue to open to my love for Sage and to learn how it could grow. My heart still belonged to Sage. It never occurred to me that love for myself could also be my intention. I had conveniently forgotten that this was my true lesson.

So I set out to fall deeper in love with Sage. In truth I was holding on. The wounds of Christmas were still fresh and the dancing although helping was not enough to soothe the pain I felt at missing Sage. The pain was deepening and I was in denial. I chose love. I went to the labyrinth many times over the week of the festival. Each time I was hoping that the magic of the ritual space would ease my pain. And some days it did. It was the place I went to for silence. There I could be still.

I found that stillness and tears are needed but to serve love is to also invite as much joy and laughter as possible. The night before New Year's Eve all the playmates dressed in costume to play. Before we headed out into the playground of the festival I dedicated the night to Sage, children, laughter and joy. That night I laughed more than I had laughed all year.

The next night as the year turned over I laughed less and reflected on what had been and what would never be again. I was in the company of my fabulous friends and playmates. Prayers and wishes were released. I was tired. Not long after midnight I slept knowing that the road was long and I had further to travel. The next day the festival was over and the playmates packed up and moved back into life and the new year ahead.

My tired limbs began to ask, "What if you stop running?" I wished to stop but had crowded my life with many things to do and a full trip back to Sri Lanka was on the agenda. There were more workshops to plan and teach, a project to launch, and my 40th birthday was on the horizon. If I had listened to the call of my heart I would have stopped running. But my head was in charge and said just keep running. I knew that I was ignoring earlier lessons; I knew that I may pay dearly for my denial, but I knew that my stubborn self would not collapse. Somewhere in there I wanted to believe that I could outrun just a slither of the pain. I bargained again with Spirit: "If I help others will you help me? Will you miraculously take some of the pain away?" I pleaded. I knew the answer. Damn that self-love shit.

BACK IN SRI LANKA The Imagine a Day Project came to life.
Sage had taught me through his imagination that anything is
possible and to honour him the project invited children to
believe in their dreams and to embrace the notion that
anything was possible. There was a bittersweet pain in
launching the project. I was beginning a relationship to a
project that honours my son. That was sweet. The bitterness
came in my knowing that the project would never be able to
hug me like Sage could. Hugs were possible but not big
squeezy hugs. I became anxious about doing the best job
possible and my anxiety grew into fear that I would fail and,
in doing so, fail Sage. On a Skype call home to Hayley she
assured me that I could not fail, that if I relaxed I would
find my way. While preparing the workshops I was torn
between feeling my fear and wishing to relax. In a moment
of surety I heard Sage tell me to imagine that he was
coming to the workshops – what is it that he would want?
FUN was the answer! I was blessed with an amazing crew
of artists who worked with me over three days to create the
inaugural Imagine a Day project workshops. I shared with
them my stories and love of Sage and I declared that fun
was our master. Through fun, open hearts and imagination
we created an experience that invited dreams and
possibilities.

The day before we facilitated the first workshops I wrote
to my family to share the story of the project and to seek
their prayers and support. My heart was bruised and needed
my family with me. The morning of our first workshops at
the Galle Children's Festival, my sister Liz replied to my

message to tell me that Sage had sent her a message via a card reading. Sage told her to tell us to eat the cupcakes. I thought this strange, given the choice, Sage would have chosen his beloved chocolate or jam donuts, not cupcakes, but I had also learnt to listen and accept. As we dressed up our workshop space with white clouds made of balloons and a mass of red balloons for fun and play, a message came from the manager of the event. Morning tea had been arranged for all the workshop leaders and it was being delivered shortly. When it arrived, I was astounded – the morning tea was cupcakes – a "without a doubt" sign. Sage was here. As a team we stopped, saluted our inspiration Sage, and set our intention on fun, dreams and possibilities.

All day children played, sang, danced and dreamed. All day I imagined Sage was with us. For the workshop my artist friend Hashita costumed up and transformed into a life-sized grandfather puppet. When the children arrived and began to play my broken heart pulsed and tears transformed to quieten my heart that delighted in my creative team and the children in full play. At the conclusion of the workshop the children sat at the feet of the grandfather puppet and one by one went to sit with him to share their dream of who they wish to be if anything was possible. One by one dreams were shared and each child was applauded. From a distance as I watched, I saw Sage sit with grandfather and tell him he was a famous inventor. That was my confirmation that what Sage wanted had come through. He was with me and breathing love and light into all those who dreamed.

I crashed after the project wrapped. For two days children had delighted in dreams and possibilities. In another few days I would turn forty. A party was being planned and whether I wanted to or not I was to attend. I didn't mind turning forty. I usually love my birthday. But the day before my birthday was outrageously painful. All through my thirties, Sage had been there. Now I was to enter a new decade and Sage was not a part of the future I was stepping toward. I made space for myself that day and walked the length of the beach to the temple that sat among the rocks at the far end. I climbed the stairs of the temple to meet with a large Buddha statue. I was awestruck by the power I felt at the top of the temple and allowed myself to crumble into the pain. I realized then that the grief at losing Sage was hard, but the building of a new life without him was a new layer of hard lessons. Love for myself had been forgotten and pushed to the end of the line in my running and creating. I was tired and facing a steep hill. I tuned in and connected to the guilt that had been sitting with me. The possibilities for my new life were endless. I knew I could carve and create what I wanted. I had the freedom of choice and could now choose all the adventures that I felt held back from as a single parent. It was possible that my new life was going to be filled with delights and adventures and I could learn to love it. I bundled up my guilt, grief, and fear, and reminded myself of what I had learned and experienced in the past year. I dusted off the debris and invited love to the party – with just a bit of sparkle.

My birthday was so much fun. The day was spent with

new and old friends. We all dressed as pirates, hired a boat and took to the seas in search of treasure. We drank, sang silly songs, and played in an imaginary world where islands were ours to steal and treasure was always on the menu. As the guilt, grief and fear ventured through the day with me, they softened and slept. It doesn't have to be heavy I was reminded. Joy and laughter are needed as much as stillness and tears.

A few weeks later I left Sri Lanka again and ventured home to the hope of a new beginning. My new beginning was sitting on a shaky foundation but I was determined and stubborn. On my way home I flew into Abu Dhabi to see my friend Adam. I arrived in Abu Dhabi but my luggage did not. Another loss. My trusty backpack that for weeks had been my turtle shell home had been filled with treasures that I felt I needed to keep close and with me on the road. I lost the compass I had bought as my connecting piece to Sage and my journey forward, a bracelet handmade by one of Sage's teachers, crystals, oracle cards and most distressing, my last Christmas gift from Sage; a wooden tree of life necklace. I was reminded of the last time my backpack had been stolen, on my trip south to Melbourne, to begin a new life, many years before. The irony was not lost. By the time I left Abu Dhabi two nights later it was clear that my bag was not to be found. My shaky foundation was now smashed open. I was tired beyond sleep and had no strength left.

"All bets are off!" I told Adam

I was now willing to let it all lay open. I was surrendering. The white flag was up and waving.

"What will you do?" Adam asked.

"I don't know. I could do anything. I could move to New York."

"Yes! Move to New York."

I knew now was not the time for answers. I let New York slip into a potential possibility.

I flew back into Australia broken. My fight to keep it all together and to rise above was over. I was now officially broken. Hayley collected me from the airport and together we drank my misery.

"What do you want to do?" she asked.

"I want to write. I want to stop."

I searched for a replacement of the tree of life necklace but found nothing. I wanted to make it all better, to buy a new one and to forget that another piece of my life had been stolen. I wanted Sage around my neck. I still wish to this day that magically it will appear and be mine again. I also wish in dreamtime that a hug from Sage could be felt and not just imagined.

BACK IN BRISBANE I continued to fall apart. I let myself fall. Relief at finally being broken. My joy in those days was Nina's son, my new godson. When I held him pieces of me came back, glued together by hope and the promise of new life. The pain and sense memory in Brisbane was overwhelming. It had been since the day I came home without Sage. My discomfort invited my running shoes back on. Where could I go to hide away from this pain? The anniversary of Sage's death was looming and I feared the turning of the tide. My new mantra arrived. "Calm the fuck down."

My wishes then came to me. Wish the best for yourself, go through the centre and into the scary places. Full circle and simple straight lines. I felt a call to be back in the mountains, to the patch of earth that Sage last shared before his exit. Circles indeed. Only three months before, at Christmas I had sworn to myself to stay away from the mountains and now it was the only place on earth I wanted to be. As I left Brisbane I cried. I was telling myself that the pain of returning without Sage was too much and that this exit must too be final. In the back of my mind I heard a whisper. "Never say never." I told that whisper to shut up and I drove my car south.

Finally I had chosen to stop. It took some time for the momentum to wind down and my mantra became a daily chant as I pulled back on my want to run. It was time to sit still. I was both relieved and scared.

I was thankful to be with my sister Kath. Her life had changed and transformed through her last year with cancer and she was pondering her new steps. Together we made a good match. I was also conscious of how little I was able to support her and other members of my family in the past year as we had all been tested and torn. My last year with grief and loss had taught me how important family and good friends are. I am immensely thankful that I have both in abundance.

I waited out the days. Each day was drawing me closer to the anniversary of Sage's death. My anxiety was high. Once again I asked myself, "How do I do this?" There seemed to be no rule book or "how to" guide. I sought to the past and what I had learnt in the first year of grief. Rituals help. Prayer helps. Accepting support from others helps. Remembering that nothing went wrong that day helps. Wishing the best for myself helps. Crying helps. Conversations with my mum and angels helps.

I decided upon 3 places of prayer. The Buddhist Temple, to honor the lessons Buddhism had taught me since Sage's passing. The Catholic Church, to honor my parents, and the Natural World to honor the support gifted silently and in earth-felt moments by trees, rivers and lakes as I wandered through grief.

On the night that marked the last day Sage was earthbound I built a ritual space around his tree in my sister's garden. I waited and watched the moon. I felt calm. As a mother, I knew my son was okay and at peace. As a mother, I knew that Sage wished me no pain and counselled me to let the sadness go. As his mother, I honoured his wish and made it my own.

The next day, the death day, I met with my three chosen places of prayer. I travelled through ritual and cried. Not for Sage, he was okay. I cried for me, for the year that had shaken me beyond belief. My love affair with Sage was alive. My love affair with myself needed some work and care. Life was granting me some time and space to stay in the mountains. I gratefully took the time and settled into the new lesson of staying still.

I dedicated to walking and writing. One step and one word at a time I was unravelling the story of water that had flowed under the bridge. I sent love to Sage daily but added a little for me also. I allowed space for dreams and possibilities for my new future to play in my mind and heart. I was not in a rush but I felt myself moving. I sensed that I would know when it was time to begin again. My need to write grew and my want for silence strengthened.

EASTER FOLLOWED CLOSE BEHIND the death day anniversary. I left the mountains and traveled to a place called Paradise Point. My friend Brains has a holiday house there and I was to meet her. We spent the first week together and the second week I spent alone, in my third silent retreat in Nature.

In the first week together with my friend, we shared stories, wine, laughter and kayak adventures on the lake. The lake at Paradise Point had come back after years of drought. When the water returned it drowned the trees on the bank. I had arrived at a place called Paradise that had an abundance of water and held a graveyard for trees. I had come to a place where not only did the water flow but when it came back it took the life of the trees in its path. I felt a great affinity to the trees. I felt an odd fear at the power of the water.

I follow the cycles of the Moon. The Moon is a great teacher and a constant reminder of the ebb and flow of life. She waxes and wanes with little effort, over and over. She brings the darkness and the light. While at Paradise the moon and sky were offering opportunity – a grand cross of planets and an eclipse were crossing the sky in the first week. Brains and I set to task. The sky was calling a ritual. On the day of the eclipse we planned and plotted. Late in the afternoon we kayaked out to a secluded point for the sunset. Once there we used the natural elements – rocks, wood and leaves – to create a ceremonial fire, and to map out the grand cross of planets. Each planet represented an element and each offered a teaching. Together we created the space and the mantra.

The heart is in the water

Freedom in the fire

Love is in the air

Earth is the path

When the site was close to ready, Brains ventured back out into the water on her kayak for one last glide before the sun set. I was invited to join her but my fear of the water stopped me. *The heart is in the water.* The strength and depth of the water seemed overwhelming and I wanted the stability of the earth, so I stayed. I pondered my fear. Our ritual was calling us to reflect upon the past two years and to then look forward. I stood in the present moment and saw clearly that despite travelling far and wide, I was still waiting for the flood waters to drown me. I was still scared. I was scared that maybe I would never move beyond grief. It was possible I would drown and become the living ghost. Again I felt an affinity with the twisted and dead trees that lined the bank of the lake. That evening I fully understood why some choose to not move away from grief. To stay with grief is to stay with the one you have lost. To stay means you are wrapped in a blanket of them.

As the sun set and into the night we walked through our ritual and reflected upon our freedom, love, and our paths. I saw all that had come before and all that was with me now.

I considered again, just for a moment, maybe I could stay here, wrapped in a blanket of Sage.

Deep into the night I realized the only way home was over the water. It was pitch black dark and the water was a large black sea, it was impossible to see where the sky began and the lake ended. My fear rose again. *The heart is in the water.* I shared my fear with my friend. Brains reassured me I was okay, and not alone. There was only one way home and together we would enter the water and glide through the dead trees. We had one torch to light our way. With encouragement and a steady grip on the torch I met the water. It was hard to see where the land became liquid so I tentatively pushed out. My heart was in my throat and I was aware that I was inhaling fear. Why am I so scared of the water I questioned? Part of me knew that my fear was not for my physical safety, it was my fear of moving away and beyond. To leave the ritual site meant I left behind the blanket. As we pushed back on the kayaks and ventured out my breath eased and I found my stride. Once out on the open water Brains said; "Turn off the torch." I thought she was mad but trusted her. Once the false light went out the true light shone brightly from above. The dark sky was littered with an abundance of stars. There above me, while sitting on top of the water, were all the possibilities, with just a little sparkle. My heart eased and filled with wonder. My heart was in the water and love was in the air. Freedom in the fire. Earth is the path.

Beyond that night I began to look forward.

In my second week at Paradise Point I was alone. The week before working on our laptops, playing music, and staying up late had drained the generator. The second day of the second week I lost power. I was truly disconnected and alone. As before in retreat I deeply reflected and allowed my full feelings to flow. Again my heart howled and the tears were heavy. The difference this time was, I knew I was moving forward. Another letting go. I began to write.

To move forward meant finding my new home. Soon it would be time to plant new seeds. I missed home but did not know where to go or how to find it. I missed having a place that was mine, a life with shape and a place to allow my full self to settle. I knew what I wanted. A new life, a new home, new possibilities, new love. It felt overwhelming. What if I made the wrong choice? Could I do this? In the silence of the week I heard Sage and my father gently easing me forward. *We are okay* they would whisper, *now you be okay. We are guiding you.*

As I drove away from Paradise Point I made peace with the water and left the dead trees behind. I was on my way back to the mountains with a determination to move forward and plant new seeds. The last day of my journey was Sage's birthday. In Heaven he would have been twelve. On the eve of his birthday I booked myself into a hotel. Sage loved to stay at hotels – the fancier the better. I booked a deluxe suite with a king size bed and spa bath. I spent the night watching movies and indulging in room service. I was sure Sage would have approved and was happy I was celebrating his birthday.

The day of Sage's birthday I woke crying and in agony. The bed was huge and swallowing me. Here I was, celebrating a birthday that was never to be. Sage was never going to turn twelve and he was not here. I would not receive or give any big squeezy hugs. No presents to open. No boy to delight in. I would never see him grow into the man I dreamed he would be.

I cried the entire day. In truth, I should not have travelled that day but I kept moving. My car sped along the highway in the hope that the next kilometre would be the one to stop the tears. I'm sure angels were on duty that day keeping me safe. I should not have been in control of a car traveling 100 km per hour. The road was teaching me that no matter how far I travel, no matter where I go, there will always be days that swallow me. I will miss Sage for the remainder of my days. There is no finishing line. No end game to play towards. I do not get to win. No matter how hard I try I will never win. I do not get my son back. I will never see him grow.

By late afternoon I arrived back in the mountains. I felt I needed more time before reconnecting with my sister and her family so I stopped at a lookout point called Govetts Leap, that reaches out over a deep valley. Back in range I checked my phone for messages. A friend and colleague of mine announced the birth of her son, born on the 5th May, Sage's birthday was now shared with another boy. Damn, another message of new life at the height of my pain. I saw an image of a bottle being thrown and smashing. I took a breath and allowed the image to pass. Since the launch of the Imagine a Day project I had a steady supply of red balloons in my bag, ready to gift a child. I reached in and grabbed one. I went to the edge of the lookout and stood among happy families and tourists and looked over the grand expanse of the mountains and valleys beyond and below. I wished the best for myself, the new child gifted life this day, and I reaffirmed my commitment to love. I blew up the red balloon, blowing my wishes and intention in with each huff. I set the balloon free.

In the wide open space I heard my heart whisper – plant more seeds, believe in the impossible dream, and move to New York City. Why not I questioned? Maybe I'll move to New York. Sage had asked me more than once if we could go to New York City. He had fallen in love with the city through the adventures of the boy lost and alone in the Home Alone 2 movie. He wished for adventures and I assured him we would go when he was older. I believed it to be true. Older for Sage never came, but I could go. I wondered for a moment if I was seeking this new plan as a soothing balm. The week before in silence and the day of Sage's birthday had left me raw. No need to rush. Allow it to naturally evolve I reminded myself.

That evening I spoke to my mother.

"Mum, I am thinking of moving to New York City."

"That sounds like a good idea," she responded with ease.

I pondered: So, if my mother thinks its a good idea, maybe it is more than a need for a new life, a rushed expectation that I will be okay and begin again, maybe this is my next home.

I began to craft my next steps. Some days I smiled. Most, but not every day I cried. Some days were ordinary. Grief and dreams sat among the ordinary everyday rhythms. On the lucky days as I walked my regular walk around the lake and through the trees I would sense Sage walking a step or two behind, gently meandering along. I began to understand that wherever I walked Sage would be there with me. My task now was to let him be and to resist holding on, to set us free. I allowed my New York City dream to become more than just a possibility. I allowed space for the ordinary to become extraordinary.

Gradually I began to see myself as a whole woman. I had accepted the image of the broken woman as me – I believed that I would one day be healed but not until the broken parts were fixed. I crafted a parachute out of all the broken pieces and saw them as simply pieces of me, perfect as they are. There was nothing to be fixed. My hurried task of trying to put myself back together had been exhausting. In truth I never really broke – I just thought I had. My heart had broken, and was still mending, but my soul had bounced and was expanding. I had been awaiting the magical moment when my task with grief would be done so I could move to the next part of the journey. I felt assured that I would know when that moment arrived. I felt that one day I would look in the mirror and see the reflection of a healed woman.

Life threw me back up north to Brisbane. I needed a job and a job was on offer. My New York dream wouldn't happen without a cash injection. Brisbane – the place that was my home, the place of my mother, where my father and son are buried, and the place that hurts the most. Damn, I thought I had just left there. *Never say never* rang in my ears as I prepared to leave the mountains and journey north again.

Before I left, in my last week in the mountains, two more deaths occurred. Two amazing women died; one who had been fighting cancer courageously, and another who suffered a freak car accident and died later with complications. The punch line of death was evident. No matter where you go or how far you travel, death is close. The only thing closer is life.

BACK NORTH IN BRISBANE I turned my attention to crafting my new beginning. I became aware that to wish myself the best was to allow the fullness of the endings before my new beginning arrived. I was surprised by the feeling of Brisbane. It didn't seem to hurt so much as I knew I was not staying long. I could see people and places from the past and feel somewhat ok, or at least numb any unpleasant feelings. I felt I had come full circle.

There was a piece of the death puzzle still missing. I had not yet received Sage's post-mortem report. I still did not know what had happened to him. I had been wishing it and dismissing it as it held great fear. It was possible that the report would reveal a fault of mine as a mother. What if there had been something I could have done to prevent his death? Had I missed something? Was I to blame? I had been told the report would take more than a year and a year had passed and the report had become a big monster in the shadows. To me, it was possible that it would arrive and reveal me as the bad mother and a new nightmare would begin.

I remembered one of my promises; go through the centre and if it is scary – but the best option on offer – I needed to do it. Continuing to wish the best for myself and with shaky resolve I sought the report. To my shock it was easy to find. I had been in denial for months and now, one phone call later, it was sitting in my inbox and one tap of a computer key and it was printed and in my hands. I was glad I was back in Brisbane. This was a familiar place. If the story turned sour I would be safe here.

Mostly I expected to find no new information. I had been

warned that testing the brain post mortem was not easy and initial reports had shown no signs of ill ease, disease or distress.

But there it was in black and white – CAUSE OF DEATH: Lymphocytic Myocarditis

What the fuck is that? The report was 32 pages of medical jargon. I was lost in my search for meaning among the words that I had no hope of pronouncing, let alone understanding. I read the words looking for the passage that said: *It's okay Deb, you did nothing wrong.* I read the words fearing the passage that said: *Bad mother! Damn her to an eternity of shame and guilt.*

Godmother Julie rang and we talked and searched for meaning together. It helped but I was not satisfied. A friend came over for a hug. It helped but I was not satisfied. I needed to know what this all meant. I needed details.

And the Universe provides again. My school friend Kate, a trained nurse and health specialist, lived close by. One message later, and she was at my door with a hug and a bottle of wine. I drank wine while Kate took me through the report. Every question I had was answered. The mystery was solved and my fear evaporated. The report revealed that there was nothing I, or anyone else, could have done to prevent Sage's death. This whole time I thought it was about the brain – his *very big brain* – but no, it was all about the heart. *Lymphocytic Myocarditis* is a rare and random condition. A virus had attacked the outer wall of his heart and it had simply stopped. No fear. No pain. Rare and random just like Sage. The whole time it was about the heart.

WEEKS LATER AND DAYS CLOSER to flying away to my new beginning in New York I was granted a gift. My computer had lost charge and I was without my charger. I had gifted Sage's laptop to my godson and I was at his house so the laptop was on offer. I opened Sage's old laptop determined to write. As I opened up the word processor it prompted me to recover a document. I wondered what it could be as obviously my godson, Mister7, was not interested in Word documents. The document I recovered and opened had been written by Sage. It was simple with straight lines. It reads;

Dear Mum I love you a lot Love Sage

A "without a doubt" sign. It's all about love – Sage's first and final lesson.

PART FOUR
The Leap

The Compass Points West.
The sun sets and surrenders to the horizon.

The Element of Water.
Our emotional body. Our Subconscious. Purification.

The Waning Moon.
"Baneful" magic – that which sends away, gets rid of, or destroys things you no longer wish to be burdened by.

LIKE A CHILD who covers their eyes, believing that if they can't see you, you can't see them, I covered my eyes and leapt forward.

When asked by strangers or soon to be new friends, why I moved to New York City, I would reply:

"I needed to jump off the cliff to see if I could still fly."

In my telling of the tale, I was being brave and flying off the cliff into the great unknown. My line, "I jumped off the cliff to see if I could still fly" was my belief. And it was true. I did want to fly. I was simply unaware that it was I who had clipped my own wings.

Innocently, like a child, I chose to believe my edited fairytale and denied the story I did not want to tell. The story of me, not facing my fears and running away – the story of my new life reality of the mother without her child. It was the triggers that I ran from. The places, people, and deep memories that held past joy and fresh pain. It was the impossible dream of moving far away from my grief I flew towards. In my flight beyond the cliff I was free from any chance encounter or trigger that may come swiftly to push my buttons of hurt. I was flying in a land devoid of all knowledge of the past and without ground.

My flight took me from my home, that was now dismantled and destroyed, to one of the biggest cities on earth, a city that guaranteed to either make you or crush you. I created a narrative of me swooping in, crafting a new life, and being as fabulous and successful as the city promises.

I did leap. I did fly. And I did crash.

Beginning again was a harder edge than I had imagined, maybe a blessing to not know, for if I had, perhaps I would have never leapt. Flying takes practice and can only be achieved by leaving the edge. I flew away and hoped that Grief was not on the flight. I had forgotten that her wings are much stronger than mine. At first I didn't like her, wouldn't let her sit with me, or hang out with my friends, but Grief dressed in black with wings that stretch far and wide enough to hold you, is a persistent bitch. She has taught me a lot. Her favourite and first teaching is "To let go." It took me many beats to learn the true meaning of this lesson.

For over a decade my life was centered around what was first, best for my son and then second, best for me. And now it was just me. I was first and had no idea where to go or what was next. After more than a year of floating, flying away, returning and grieving, I had convinced myself that the only way to a new life was to leap. I was sure that if I did not leap off the cliff of possibility I would begin to slowly disintegrate into a form unrecognisable to me; the grieving mother who conjures up pity and awkward social exchanges. I had grand ideas of a new beginning that would somehow create a world that would take the pain away and would give me a new purpose. I would be the gorgeous and powerful heroine in my new story.

Once in New York City, I felt much like Alice down the rabbit hole. I was in a strange land, without grounding, surrounded by characters and mixed messages. I was seeking my way home and was unsure where or how to find it. I was not fabulous or successful. I was sad and lost.

I began to understand why Alice spent so long down the rabbit hole seeking her way home. It was confusing, painful, at times shocking, and definitely filled with twists of fate. I was not home, but had arrived at my new home, and I had never felt so alone. Even in the days after Sage had passed I was at times alone but did not feel alone. I was now surrounded by hundreds and thousands of people who all knew their way around Wonderland and I was lost. In the early days I asked myself more than once: "What have you done? Why did you leap? How did you ever think this was a good idea?"

My grief was at a new intensity and raw. I felt the pressure of expectation to start over. I missed Sage and I was scared. Denying one story and crafting another was not a straight line to healing or in any way helpful, but I had arrived and was determined.

As an Australian/American, I foolishly thought my new life in America would be easy to craft. Days into my crash landing I caught the subway to Lower Manhattan to visit the social security office. I was on a mission to get my social security number, the magic digits that would open up my possibilities: a new job, apartment, bank account, US phone number, all the essentials to adult reality. My number is called and I arrive at the small window armed with my US birth certificate and valid passport, believing a signed form later would grant me my number and I could step out into the city as someone ready to begin again. My documents are viewed and my form is read.

"Have you lost your number?" I am asked

"No, I have never had one."

A puzzled expression crosses the face of the teller behind the window "Why?"

"I have never worked in the US and so have never needed one."

"So where have you been?" I am viewed as an alien.

"I grew up in Australia and have lived most of my life there."

"Most of your life....?" The question hangs in the unknown.

"Yeah, I have traveled a bit also."

"Oh." The teller turns and leaves. Deeper behind the window I see her talking to another and gesturing in my direction. I have no idea what is going on, I begin to get an unsettling feeling in my belly that points toward trouble.

Upon return the trouble is dished out. "We are going to need you to prove where you have been starting from five years old, in a maximum of two year increments."

"Prove? How?"

"Medical records, school reports, proof of employment. We need the evidence on letterhead, signed in wet signature."

"Wet?"

"Yes, originals signed. Hardcopies. No emails or fax documents."

"But, I'm a citizen, I have a valid passport. I have been granted more than one US passport over the years. My mother is American, four of my siblings have lived and worked here." I am clutching at the air for a thread of hope.

"Original documents, wet signatures, maximum two year increments." The cold lack of hope descends and slides down the small window barrier. I stand in shock and wait for an alternative plan. There is no alternative, no other way out. The next number is called and I am cast aside. My task now, according to the US government, is to prove who I am and where I have been.

I walked away and into the busy streets of Manhattan with a burning that was eroding any strength I had left. I was now officially lost and sat in a dark hole scratching the surface in search of the answer to who I was and where I had been. I spent days sitting in the small room I shared with my sister Heather and stared out the window into my new world or cried. My grief for Sage was now weighed down by my own sense of loss. I had leaped off the cliff and was in a fast flailing freefall. I expected the earth to come meet me, but it didn't. I just kept falling.

THREE WEEKS after I arrived in New York, Halloween arrived complete with its haunting. As it was my first Halloween in the US, I didn't know of its intensity, rhythm, and traditions. I did not expect the children till after dark. I thought I could avoid the trick or treating. I ventured out of the apartment on a mission to go to a store close by on a busy street filled with dollar stores, mom and pop shops, and a few cafes and restaurants. A simple task I thought. It was late in the afternoon and the school bell had rung to release many children of all sizes out into the streets dressed in costumes and wide grins, in search of the candy that followed the prompt, "Trick or Treat." Each and every child, happy and prancing, felt like red hot daggers. It was surreal to be the one among many who felt the pain and not the joy. The true depth of the pain was in my memory of the last Halloween I had spent with Sage. The year that followed our magical Halloween in our street was our last Halloween together. Days before our last night of potential tricks or treats Sage had asked if we could again knock on doors in costume. I was busy; projects were piling up, the mortgage was due, and I felt tired all the time. With little regard for the enormity of my words I told Sage yes, we could. And then I promptly forgot. Our last Halloween together was a terror known to parents; the look of pain on your childs face, the pain you know you have caused. That last Halloween I arrived home late, tired, with more work to do before rest was mine. As I went through the motions of cooking vegetables and wishing upon wine to numb away reality, Sage pranced into the kitchen and asked when he could begin to get ready.

"Ready for what?" I ask without looking up to meet his eye.

"The trick and treating. It's Halloween, remember?"

"Oh, we can't do that. We didn't send the notes, no one is expecting us, it's too late Sage." I can't remember if I looked up as I delivered the news, but I do remember thinking that I was tired and hated stupid holidays that put pressure on parents. My jaw tightened as I stirred the vegetables.

"But, you said yes." The tremble heard in Sage's voice is what stopped me. I looked up to see his pain seeking the turnaround moment that he so wanted. The moment I, as his mother, drop everything and bring back the magic. Instead of dropping, I clenched the spatula and broke his heart.

"Well Sage, sometimes a yes one day is a no the next day. Life is not always fair." My words were harsh, but the true stab was in my nasty tone.

Tears gleaned the lower lids of Sage's eyes and he left slowly with his head dipped down in hurt. I stood in the kitchen with rising anger at myself, and at the pressure I felt. Here I was again, stirring vegetables, and being not enough, with nobody to pick up the spatula and ensure the vegetables are eaten, nobody to cover the next mortgage payment, and the only one who could break my son's heart the way I had.

I found Sage sitting on the red couch. I sat with him and after his breath settled I spoke. "Sage, I'm sorry."

"I really wanted to go. You said, yes."

"I know. I'm sorry." Sorry was all I had.

Sage turned to me and, with slow steady tears, melted into my arms. I held him and hated myself. We sat for some time saying nothing, and then into the silence Sage said:

"It's ok mum." Even with his own heart broken Sage was able to hold mine.

The next day I took Sage to the store and told him he could choose whatever candy he wanted. He danced his happy dance and took his time selecting his sugar treasures. I promised myself that day that I would do better at being Sage's mum, that I would keep promises, care less about the things that don't really matter, and I was damn sure that the next Halloween was going to be bigger and better than Sage could imagine. Never getting the chance to repair a tear in your child's heart is a pain that never goes away.

ONE DAY IN NOVEMBER, after the horror of Halloween and with the building tension of looming Christmas, I returned to what I know: writing, meditation and movement. Each morning I would write, attempt stillness in meditation, and every day I forced myself to leave the apartment, even if it was to simply walk around the block. Some days, a walk around the block was all I could muster.

It took almost three months to get all the documents needed and to be gifted my number. My social security card arrived days before Christmas. A flimsy paper, not quite cardboard slip, with the digits to my destiny. It was the only present I wanted that year and I felt great relief when I tore open the envelope.

The day before my forty-first birthday, on the last day of January, I trudged through a blizzard of sideways snow across Brooklyn to sign a lease to the new apartment that would become the Driscoll sisters' base. Pieces were falling into place and my writing and meditation were delivering slithers of peace and the actual hope that one day soon I would be okay and my new life would take shape. In order to get the apartment I said yes to the first job offered. A lease credit check required payslips so I said yes to the pain of being with children. That winter I was the new after-school drama activity specialist at a Brooklyn Primary School. Each day of the school week I would catch the three subway rides it took to get to the school. Most days I sat in a crowded carriage and cried. Going to be with children everyday was so incredibly painful, but I was determined to not bring my pain into the school and into their worlds, so I would cry my way to work to release the tears. Close to my stop I would wipe my face, apply lipstick and force a fake smile. The children in the after school program were all young and innocent, some naughty and some lost. The one thing they had in common was their desire to be met by a loved one as the school bell rang and to be scooped up and taken home. Instead their school day stretched to 6pm and their energy would twist to either tears, tantrums, or mischief. There was a group of boys that were particularly naughty and a few young ones who were obviously different and struggling. I found myself gravitating towards the naughty and different. It was sad to watch the young bodies digest the crappy sugar and salt laden packaged food they were given as their snack, and sadder to watch the sugar-hyped kids being yelled at for not standing still in line. It was absurd, akin to giving ecstasy to a raver and then telling them to not dance to the music.

I wanted to quit, but I wanted an apartment more and desperately needed the pay slips and the US dollars. Weeks into my job I sensed the lesson of why I had been given this job. I was being taught to take the long road, to not quit or runaway, to be patient and invite children in, and to stay on the train and sit in my pain. I heard the message and gritted my teeth. I turned my attention to the children rather than my pain and I began to see a new way for us to be. The naughty boys I challenged with fun physical tasks and adventures, the different kids I sat with longer at break time to hear their long-winded stories, and I chose to not yell. I made a silent promise to the children that I would be the one who never yelled at them and who would listen to what their difference or mischief was trying to express. If a class I was teaching became raucous or unfocused I would bring stillness and taught the children mindfulness meditation. I ensured I told them this was not a punishment, but simply a different way of being. In truth, they didn't like the meditation, they liked the play. As time went on we played more and sat still less.

By Spring I had a new job and was able to say goodbye to the three subway rides, the poor pay rate and sadly to the children. I had grown fond of them and had taken a shine to more than one young soul sitting out the afternoons till hometime. On one of my last days I sat with Lucas, a young boy that reminded me a lot of Sage. Lucas had his own way of being in the world and was tuned to a different vibration. I often sat with him to calm him when the noise of the many children became too much. I chose to tell him that I was leaving, as I knew he needed to know. To one day arrive and not see me, for me to disappear, would have been disturbing for him. He asked if I would be coming back. When I told him no he said, "Well you can come to my house to play. And you can bring your son." I had not told anyone of Sage, not the teachers or the children. I sat in silence with Lucas and let Sage simply be there with us. I didn't question further or ask why he thought I had a son, I took a moment to be with Lucas and with the son he knew I had.

At my new job, a human rights and storytelling nonprofit, I met people more like me who had stories to share and new places and events I could enjoy in the city. I listened to their stories and chose not to tell my own. I became the woman who moved to the city from Australia – full stop. The mother in me was nowhere to be seen by others, except for a select few I trusted. I blended into the rhythm of the city. I worked hard at my new job, I began dating (unsuccessfully, but that's a different story), and I merged further into the narrative of me, just a woman, not the me that was the grieving mother. I ignored grief, except for when alone at home. There she raged. I would lock myself away to cry and spent whole days in a trance of pain. My sister Heather was the only witness. When asked by people at work how my weekend was I would lie. I had convinced myself that my new life needed to be devoid of grief so I shut her out of any and all places that my new life had breath. I began ending my day by drinking and found peace from my pain among the many New Yorkers who sought out happy hour at the end of the work day.

Sage and his presence was felt by me throughout the city and it was with my sister Heather that it felt like he was allowed. Heather would care for me when I fell down the rabbit hole. At first we were both at a loss with my new layer of grief, but Heather has an amazing, generous and practical heart, and with patience she found a way to send a bucket down the rabbit hole with a pulley, so from a distance I could be reached. Heather and I delighted in dandelions, which blossom around the time of Sages birthday, and white feathers, two signs to us that Sage was close by, and it was with Heather that I would visit the Plaza Hotel, my "Sage Place" in the city, to sit in The Rose

Club, sipping champagne and making wishes. With Heather, Sage was given life in New York.

THE SECOND ANNIVERSARY of Sage's death I spent time in the countryside of Massachusetts at my new boss' country home. Heather and I built an altar out by a tree and I spent time laying on the grass and feeling the sun on my face. I was not at peace and felt the disturbance of my heart. Rather than relax I berated myself for not moving on, for wallowing in self pity, for not doing better. I decided there were no excuses left and it was time to get over it. My soul moulded into a shield and I set about the task of raging through the pain in an attempt to eliminate it before it could destroy me. My Driscoll resolve rose to the surface and I picked up my sword and ran into battle with myself. I was determined to find grief and cut her out of my life, as she was my enemy and the one who reminded me and taunted me that my son was gone. I never found grief on the battle ground, but I did find myself, not as a warrior but a woman who was tired and wished her life away.

I found my battle ground in the streets of New York. I had a new relationship to traffic and death. I was no longer the driver, I was the pedestrian. In busy Manhattan Avenues, rushed New Yorkers walk out beyond the curb in their haste to cross the street. I quickly blended into the rhythm of the foot traffic. My raw and ignored grief rebirthed my wish to magically die. While out walking I would without looking, step out into traffic. I began to play a game of chance. Thoughts of the driver conveniently forgotten.

It was only when the fantasy became possible, when it was clear I was not winning the battle, that I surrendered and again confessed. Each confession was a step toward staying alive and earthbound. Beyond the confession were therapy sessions and a return to my commitment of daily spiritual practice. The death desire turned down in volume to a low ebb of thought that screeched out loud on an odd day that grief was in force.

Deep into my days in New York, on Sage's thirteenth birthday, I wandered in the cold through Washington Square Park with nowhere in particular to be or go, but with a need to be out in the vibe of the city. In a slip of a moment, between thoughts, I sensed again the Middle Eastern guide who had come to visit me in my dreams days before Sage died.

"Remember, the research is important."

It then became obvious. I am the research – my life, the loss of my lover, my father and my son. I have been researching and learning for years. Grief is my master teacher and over the years I have been taught layers of lessons. I could hear the message. I knew a new layer of its meaning, but I did not feel strong enough to do anything about it. Loss was slicked under my skin and I felt at purpose with my learnings and sorry for myself at the same time. This mix stalled all movement forward except for my knowing that death has had a reason in my life and one day the research will mean something.

MY SECOND HALLOWEEN IN NEW YORK is when Grief came out to play. I chose to be her. I dressed in black and adorned my back with wide black wings. At a warehouse party deep in Brooklyn I danced as Grief, and let her out to be seen. The next day I picked Grief and her wings up off the floor and placed them on top of my tall dresser of drawers facing my bed. It was a purposeful move, it was time to stare Grief down.

Many months after the leap, and after many adventures, I found the answer to my questions of the early days. New York City is as big as my grief. By surviving the city I was surviving grief. I had taken my hands away from my eyes, allowed myself to be seen, and was looking towards a new landscape and the crafting of my new life.

ON THE THIRD ANNIVERSARY of Sage's death I traveled to Kosovo to work on The Imagine a Day Project, the project I had created for Sage and launched in Sri Lanka. It was time again to invite the children of the world to imagine a day and to believe in their impossible dreams. I was with my creative companion, Hayley, who had secured the funding and created the opportunity for me, and a team from her university in the UK. We worked for two weeks with a group of twenty teachers, youth leaders and community workers, who all wished to create a new future, for themselves and the children and youth they worked with. Years of conflict had, as wars do, caused great divide and pain in the country. They openly engaged in our process and project and began to see how the imagination can be a magical force that can shift pain to possibility. It was a great privilege to work with them.

I was swimming in a myriad of emotions. Working on the project, while beautiful, was also a reminder that Sage was dead. The waves of grief began to pick up momentum and I worked hard at standing my ground in the tumultuous waters. Halfway through our two weeks in Kosovo the third death day came crashing and the pain won at crushing me. I floundered with my deep missing of Sage and wanted desperately to move away from pain and be available to the people I was working with and serving. All I knew then of moving away and letting go was to move away from him, to let Sage go. I held on and the pain stayed as I was dunked under high waves that kept coming. In the throes, I again missed a narrative playing out in front of me. My friend Hayley was unwell and needed me. I knew this and turned my attention to the work and the project, and missed the beat that was calling my attention to the heart of my friend. Hayley had cared for me so deeply over my years without Sage and it hurt just as deep when it was revealed that I had not been there to support her in the way she needed. Our years of friendship helped to hold us as we both collapsed. I was angry at myself, and angry at grief for stealing my perspective and creating a tunnel vision of survival.

Days after the anniversary and at the completion of the project I heard a new message. Sage's repeated message transformed from "Go Mum" to "Let me go Mum."

I sat with Hayley on our last day in Kosovo and shared my feelings and the message. In my telling of the new message an image appeared. In my mind's eye I saw my palms open and the space around me shift from closed to expansive. In the space created a flood of children swam in. The image was colorful, dynamic, and filled with innocence and delight. It brought tears to my eyes and my whole being.

I left Kosovo with a heavy heart and the sensation of assurance that new layers of grief were coming and I was unsure of what would happen next. As I sat with the image in the weeks that followed, it inspired a direction forward of service and the opening towards others. I reflected on the many missed moments that grief had stolen and I allowed my shame to sit with me. It was not immediate but over time, I released shame and guilt and said sorry to those I had hurt or denied in my years of swimming in the crazy waters of grief. I followed the pulse of this new message, and I began the embodied process of letting go.

THE ORGANIZATION I WORKED FOR was based at a co-working space that was managed by a dynamic team. One member of the team, Lucy, pulled me aside one day to tease my interest in a program that was soon to be on offer at the space. The offer was to be in the first circle of women to pilot a new program called A Fearless Force. The program invites a group of women to craft signature speeches. Being with women, check. Crafting stories, check. Public speaking and signature speeches, check. Me on stage, in a frock with a microphone in hand, check. The opportunity felt engaging and I was pleased Lucy had chosen me as one of the potential women. It all sounded great to me, until I asked when.

"The first weekend in May will be the workshop and then during the week you work with Eduardo and on Thursday night is the public event where all the women take to the stage to share their speeches."

That Thursday in May hung heavy and in a swift swirl, a ball of fear cramped the space between Lucy and myself. The Thursday was Sage's birthday and to me, the most painful day of the year. I shifted in my seat in search of a comfort that was slipping away as I felt the fear grow in strength.

"Lucy, that Thursday is my son's birthday."

"Oh, do you have plans? Maybe he could come."

I took a deep breath and expelled the sorrow that was making friends with the fear between us.

"My son died three years ago. On the 5th of May, he would have been celebrating his 14th birthday."

219

Lucy leaned forward and in that move she shifted the fear between us and a new feeling opened up. "I didn't know. Deb, I'm sorry." Sitting with the discomfort, but now feeling the possibility of being supported, I saw the opportunity I was being gifted. Lucy sat with me while I explored what it would be like, to work on a speech that shared my grief, that revealed the full and real me, and again brought Sage to center stage and in focus. I remembered my third wish to myself in the early days: to go through the center and if it is scary but the best way through, I was to do it. I swallowed the fear and said yes.

The weekend workshop was amazing, painful, heart-opening and challenging. In the company of seven other fearless and fantastic women, and under the steady guidance of Eduardo and his partner coach Ben, we crafted our stories. In the process I was able to find new nuances to my experience and chose to focus on Sage as my master teacher. What emerged was a love story of grief in action, a story of me giving all the love I have for Sage to the world.

On the 5th of May I woke in tears as I had every 5th of May without Sage. The difference being this year I had a speech to practice, a rehearsal to get to, and by sundown I was to be on stage sharing my story. I hid in the apartment for the morning and let all the ugly tears out and wondered if I could do it, if I could stand and deliver. I was unsure if I could leave the apartment. I considered the wings, the big black wings that hung in my bedroom. Should I wear them? Is a costume going to give me the courage I need? The answer was no, it was not Grief that was to take the stage, it was me, flawed and all. I chose a black tutu skirt I had bought in Kosovo and felt closer to ready. The last ingredient, glitter, pushed me out the door and onto the subway. With just a little bit of sparkle I stood on stage that night, vulnerability shaking through me. I cried and stumbled, more than once. It was not perfect, but it was exactly what I needed to open my heart and feel safe sharing my full story, ugly tears, glitter, and all.

ONE ORDINARY DAY in Manhattan I sat with my boss, Talia, our intern Dan, and the lawyer of our board, Edward. Easy conversation flowed and Edward shared a story of one of his grandchildren. I add in my own similar experience with Sage and it prompts the question that stops the flow.

"How old is your child?" Edward asks.

Talia quickly side-glanced at me and Dan looked lost and confused. Stories of Sage had never been at work before. My want to stare down and go public with Grief had brought Sage into my everyday conversations and this was a moment I was having again and again in my new version of New York. Those who had known me now for almost two years were learning of my past, my son, and his death. Each time Sage and Grief came into the everyday it was both uncomfortable and eased my discomfort at the same time. Little by little my guard was pulled away and both Grief and Sage came into the light.

One of the women in the Fearless Force program opened her speech by sharing her experience of running into the freezing water dressed as Wonder Woman, at Coney Island on New Year's Day at the Annual Polar Bear Plunge. Inspired by her, (she truly is a Wonder Woman!), I decided to also plunge. On New Year's Day 2017, three-and-a-half years after Sage's death, I dressed in my Grief wings and took Grief for a plunge into freezing water. It was time Grief was given a salt bath cleanse and a reset. With my sister Heather there as my forever support partner, we ran into the freezing waters as drums roared and people cheered. Once in the water I lay back to soak the wings. I thanked Grief for all her teaching, her support and for holding me when I couldn't hold myself. I stayed in the water longer than most as it felt like the time was needed to truly let go. That afternoon I partied on the boardwalk with my sister, I hugged my Wonder Woman friend, and I wore my wings with pride. The next day I moved the wings down into the basement storage unit in our building.

I felt into the spaces between and around me, I created expansion and called in new experience. I began to focus on myself and what being in the world meant to me. I shifted to a service frame of mind and wondered what gifts I had to share and how could I be of use and benefit to others. I welcomed back the children I had kept at arm's length. Gently and slowly, the world around me and within me transformed.

ON THE FOURTH ANNIVERSARY of Sage's death I sat alone on a beach in Jamaica. I had five days to sit, write, feel and cry. The few employees at the small family-owned guest house I was staying at were the only people I spoke to for the five days, and most of that was to ask Mrs. K for another Red Stripe beer, to request my meal from Chef Smith, or to say good morning to the day guard, Dave, and good evening to the night guard, Tim. It was not a joyous holiday, but it was just what I needed. The time away from the loud beat of New York gave me the space to feel deep into my being and to reflect. I wrote many love letters to the people who had supported me over my years of loss and I wrote letters to my grief, anger, shame and guilt. The letters were not intended to be sent, but they did need to be written. At sunset of the fifth and last day I stared out to the far horizon. The water was calm and the horizon formed a straight line far in the distance that blended without effort the sea and the sky. It was then I realized I could see my own horizon and it was as wide as the sky and as deep as the sea. I had been looking and trusting only a few steps ahead in my journey since leaping to New York. I was still scared I would crash and Grief kept my tunnel vision focused on what was directly ahead. And now, the wide horizon beckoned me forward.

It was around that time when I also realized that I had neglected the witch in me. I had not taught any Reiki courses, treated anybody, and was dimming down my intuition with rivers of wine and pints of beer. The wide horizon on the beach in Jamaica showed me my own horizon invited magic and was full of possibilities. I began to invite my witch back.

I embraced Grief as my friend and teacher. I let her sit with me long enough to hear her. She told me that it is in the letting go, in the creation of space, that we allow new layers to develop so she can, in concert with us, work on heart repair and soul expansion. I nurtured my relationship with Grief and spent as much time with her as I did with the spirit of Sage. In truth, I think Sage was relieved. When I would call on him to meet me in the space between worlds he would tell me I was okay, he was okay, and also he was busy and had things to do. A true teenage boy response. It was Grief who was pleased to see me. She was so happy I had surrendered and was allowing time and space to learn from her.

In my search for the balance point of grief, I over-indulged in what I imagined was joy. I spent a lot of time out in the city, drinking, sharing stories, and having random love affairs. This pattern of allowing grief had created a new pattern of self-medicating and my self prescribed medicine of alcohol wasn't enough so I searched for love and pain relief in a handful of strangers. I was doing so well at being with my grief, that it took me a long time to realize my behaviour was destructive to my being and my own version of self-punishment that had been with Sage before his death. Once I saw this I could not ignore it.

ON NEW YEAR'S EVE OF 2017 I sat with my good friend Rasheed in a bar in Queens. We chugged beer and mused over the year that was passing. I invited us to play a game of kiss, marry or kill. It's a game you play where three people are pre-selected and you have to decide who you are going to kiss, marry or kill. I twisted the game to meet the new year's tradition of resolutions and invited us to think of parts of our lives we would kiss, marry or kill. I kissed opening my life up to new job possibilities, and I married writing the book I knew I was ready to write. My kill was easy to declare as I knew it needed to die. I killed the random love affairs and swore I would not kiss another man unless I actually liked him and truly wanted to. Time for punishment was over. Self-love had finally arrived at the party.

One day, early into the new year, I sat in meditation and invited Sage to meet me. I was in a garden with a stone bench in the center and surrounded by tall stone walls and an open gate. I sat on the bench and waited. When Sage arrived he was wearing all white and walked through the gate with a new authority I had not seen in him before in visions. When I stood to hug him I marveled at the feeling of reaching up to him, he was now taller than me. My son was growing up in spirit. Sage and I sat together on the stone bench and it brought sense memories forward of our days together on the red couch. In time Sage spoke.

"We are happy with your new direction and commitment to self-love. We are pleased you have begun to write the book. You are on the path now. But Mum, it was never planned for you to be on this path alone. Partnership is possible, but it is up to you to choose it."

When Sage left it was for me, too soon, but I watched him walk away without pulling him back. I sat on the bench for sometime and questioned whether I would risk my heart again. Journeying alone was a choice I could make that felt safer. Mike's words from years before rang in the air. Maybe he wasn't right, maybe it did not have to be lonely. I remembered to wish the best for myself.

ON THE FIFTH ANNIVERSARY of Sage's death, I sat in meditation at a retreat in the mountains of Massachusetts. It was day six of a ten-day silent Vipassana retreat. I had purposefully chosen to be still and silent as I was seeking a new way of being on this day. For the remainder of my earthbound days, the 3rd of April, the horror day of the year will arrive. That I could not change, but my depth of hurt on that day I could. I was unsure if a new way could be found but I was a keen seeker and had chosen surrender. When I woke that day I couldn't believe I had thought this was a good idea. The retreat, as well as being silent, asked the meditators to not gesture, avoid eye contact, and absolutely no physical contact. My nightmare day of the year had arrived and I could not hug anyone, was separated from everyone who loved me, and was unable to scream. All in attendance were supervised and supported by master teachers. The two teachers, one for the men and the other for the women, sat at each meditation in the great hall and silently guided. If extra guidance was needed you requested time in a break to sit with the teacher for ten minutes. That morning in meditation my back had begun to twitch in the way it does just before it snaps out of balance. I made an appointment that afternoon to see the teacher to request a supportive stool. It was the one moment I had that day with eye contact and words shared.

"Debra, I am so glad you requested to see me today," were the opening words from my teacher. I sat opposite her, holding back tears. "I read in your application that today is a hard day for you."

"Yes, it's the fifth anniversary of my son's death. My back is hurting today, hurting in the way it does just before it goes out."

"You need support. Let me assign you a back-supported stool."

"Thank you. I do need the support. I am seeking a new way of sitting with this day."

"You are in the storm Debra. When in a storm out at sea, you seek your anchor."

"My anchor?" I question.

"Yes, your breath. Take each breath and allow each to anchor you. It is the only way to survive the storm."

Surrendering to each breath was the key to finding my answer. After breakfast and lunch each day we were given the option to rest, return to meditation, or to walk in the forest on a designated path. I always chose the forest. The afternoon of the anniversary I reflected on what the master teacher had taught in the lessons over the evenings of the course. He taught one evening of life paths and how there are more than one, and he laughed at the idea of loss of life, as he didn't see it that way. What he saw was a soul, after death, graduating to their next level of soul experience. With trees as my witness the graduation day of Sage came alive and a broad smile spread across my face and my heart sang with pride. My son, Sage, the master teacher, famous inventor and wise old man, had graduated early. My son became an overachiever in soul lessons and graduated before the rest of his class. My breath deepened and I spent the rest of the day feeling into my new way of being on the 3rd April, now known as Sage's graduation day.

I spent the remaining four days looking forward into my wide horizon and deep sky of possibility. My graduation day was years away and I had choices with how I would live out those days. In the silence, I spent time with my learning of grief and death, and I sat with the pockets of hurt that needed healing. I sat with the expansive possibilities of my life and unearthed my secret desire to die. My wish to die by magic had diminished and lay under cold coals, mostly unfelt by me. One stir of the coals revealed the embers that lay under the cold grey debris. I have always been mystified with how long it takes a burning fire to cool and be forever ash. The desire had not been felt for a long time but upon discovery, I found that it lay just under the surface and I was holding on, just in case my grief needed the fantasy.

It was in my repeated return to breath in meditation that I made a new commitment and began crafting a way forward down a new road. I decided that in order to survive and then thrive in the years I had left in earth time without Sage, I needed to release and extinguish the death desire. I promised myself that I would place my focus on being alive and earthbound and creating a life that could be joyous without Sage. I balanced my grief with the potential of an open heart. I was choosing to live a big life and to be the white witch healer I am.

DAYS AFTER THE RETREAT I flew south to the Caribbean. The year before on Sage's birthday my friend Phoebe had secured precious funding that gifted her the opportunity of ten months in Trinidad and Tobago to work on a project of birth stories. Feeling tired as I trudged through the city in the five weeks between Sage's death day and his birthday, I had decided that the following year I would take time off to be with my grief. At the time I was unsure of how life would be rearranged to manage the time off from the normal rhythm of work, but I committed to making what seemed impossible, my reality. As Phoebe was to be in the sun I chose to fly to her.

Early in the New Year, in a dream, I saw a veranda that overlooks a large body of water. In the dream, I knew it to be my writing spot. The next morning I woke with the image clear in my mind and took it as a sign that it was time to google possibilities of where I would stay when I flew south. I had been successful in carving out weeks to be and write, and to sit by water as the next birthday of Sage's passed in earthtime without him. My google search pulled up pictures of a guest house that had images of its veranda, and those images were the pictures in my dream, my writing spot! The guest house is located on the island of Tobago. I was not intending to visit Tobago, I was planning my time in Trinidad, but this was a "without a doubt" sign and one not to be ignored. I booked a three-week stay and arrived introducing myself as Debra, the writer, and in time to a few as Debra, the writer, and white witch healer.

Sitting on the veranda after sunset on my second day at Millers Guest House I spoke to my mother on video chat. She was hours away from being admitted for major surgery to cut out part of her left lung and had chosen the option of minimal care and no extreme measures if her health failed or the surgery was unsuccessful. I knew of my mother's plan for her care and I supported it. It was uncomfortable, but I knew her reasonings and I knew given the choice, I would also choose to allow it to be and let go. She was clear about the peace she felt with her life and was choosing to either live fully or not at all. She did not want to be hooked up to machines or under the constant care of others. She was also at peace with meeting again her husband and soulmate, her father, and Sage. I understood that desire. As we spoke she asked me how I was and I without a hesitant beat replied:

"Mum, I think I'm ready to meet someone." This was music to my mother's ears. She asked me when Sage died to not close my heart, and although I was able to hear her request, I was not able to follow. My broken heart had stayed connected to Sage and denied entry to another.

"Ok, so what are you looking for? What type of partner?"

"Mum, fuck the list. The list of who I thought I should be with has never led me to love."

"Ok, so what do you want?"

"I just want someone who likes me, and I like them."

"That'll work."

I thought deeper into my wish and saw what it was missing. "And Mum, they must have a good heart."

It felt risky to ask for love when my mother was going

into surgery, that she would either survive or would end her days. The last time I had asked for an opening of my heart and for love had been the precursor to Sage's death. It felt risky but it also felt different this time. I was learning a lot about the capacity of the heart, had found peace with my past, and begun the lifelong process of self-love. I went to sleep that night praying my mother would be okay and that my wish would come true.

The next morning at dawn I woke. I made myself a cup of coffee and gathered up my journal to venture out to the large veranda to watch the rising sun. The veranda overlooks a jetty where the local fishermen dock their boats and cut up their fish. In the early light of the day I see a man at the fish table carving up wood. He is tall with long dreads and strong muscles that flex and lengthen with each stroke of the knife. I watched his shirtless back as he carved out a new fishing hook. 'What a pleasing way to start the day,' I thought. The man turns and upon seeing me waves hello. I wave back and a connection is made.

Later that day as I wandered to the close-by beach a truck slowly pulls up beside me. As I peek inside the open window of the vehicle I see the man from the jetty.

"You going to the beach?" he asks

"Yes," I reply and increase my pace. I wasn't sure why, but staying to speak to him made me nervous.

After my swim and on my way back to the guest house I pass the local beach bar and see a man running towards me across the open beer garden. It is the man from the jetty. He bounces up to me with a broad smile.

"This is the third time I have seen you today and I still do not know your name."

I tell him my name, he shares his and our hands meet in the exchange of our third hello. As we stand there our hands hold each other longer than necessary and the nervous feeling I had shifted to a feeling of, oh my, this could be trouble, in the "I'm going to want to kiss this man" kind of trouble.

"Tonight a few of us will be playing drums by the beach bar. You should come."

"Oh, I am not sure what I am doing tonight. I am waiting on news from home. My mother is having surgery today. By tonight I may not feel like being out."

"Don't sit alone. Be with us."

I hesitated in thought. Being close to him felt like a warm fire that comforts rather than burn. I wanted to move closer. He offered more.

"I'll tell you what, if you come, I will play drums for your mother."

"Okay, maybe." As I leave, I know that it will not be the drums that pull me out that night but my desire to see him again.

As the sun set that day I felt very alone and fear sat with me on the veranda of my writing spot as I downed a cold beer. Here I was, on a small island very far away from everyone who knew and loved me and the day may end with bad news from home. Over the sea and sitting on boats in front of me were many small pelicans. I sat with my father and his memory and prayed for good news from home.

The drums did pull me out that night but I didn't stay long as my need to be in wifi range to get word from home was greater than my need to stay close to the man drumming for my mother.

The next day I learn my mother survived surgery and was in recovery. It was the man on the jetty who hugged me as I felt into my relief.

"See, I told you. I told you it was all going to be okay," he assured me.

Days later we stood high on a cliff and watched the sun set, followed by the rising of the full moon. In the light that is left after a setting sun, he kissed me. To him, I am a witch, to me, he is a werewolf. Opposites in the world of magic but a match for challenge, growth, and a slice of trouble.

Months into my stumble and tumble with the werewolf I saw Sage in a meditation. He sat with me and said: "Mum, I am sorry for breaking your heart. It is time now to love again."

I had worked so hard at putting my heart back together that taking the risk of sharing it with another felt overwhelming. I sat with my fear, Sage's words, and my heart. In time I saw all the magic possible if I surrender my heart to love. Sure, it may get broken, but where is the magic of life if our hearts are hidden and protected? My lessons along the path had taught me that our hearts have capacity far beyond our fear and humans seek connection not only because it feels good, but because we need it. There lies the magic. To risk your heart is breathing life into the hope of big love. A life lived in big love means you will grieve, you will grow, you will touch joy. Not everyone we love we get to keep, but while they share time with us, we can choose to love them.

For I now know, without a doubt, that one day you may wake and a loved one doesn't, you may swerve and just miss the oncoming truck, you may meet a soulmate in the strangest of places, you may leap off a cliff, and you may, if lucky, let go and surrender.

The End and The Beginning

The Medicine Wheel.

The interconnectedness of humans and nature, cycles and spirals of energy. The physical embodiment of our spiritual energy, an outward expression of our internal relationship with Spirit.

All cardinal directions of the compass, in flow with the phases of the moon, the gifts of the elements, and turning to the vibration of the beating heart.

GRIEF FOR ME HAS BEEN A SERIES OF SURRENDERS. When you relax with her, Grief will show you tenderness. She has become one of my friends.

Grief can only be felt if love is there first. The trouble with Grief is you cannot make new memories, put her to bed, check to see if the homework is done or ensure enough vegetables are eaten. Grief will not walk you down the aisle on your wedding day or hold your children when they are born. But Grief will sit with you and remind you that you love.

Lessons in love are taught every day. I am learning to turn up to the class and be open to the lessons. I forever hold space in my heart for Nick, my Father, and Sage, and thank them for their time and gifts they granted me in earth time, and through Spirit in the time that passes beyond a death.

I am thankful that some lessons and wisdom were granted before Sage passed, so that I could be in earthtime with him and enjoy the deepening of our love and understanding. Some days I am sad that so much of my learning has come due to the shift taking place after Sage left, and I wish I had known more when in early grief of Nick and my Father. I remind myself that we can only ever know what we know when we know it, and when we are ready to receive the lesson. On those days, I remind myself that I am still with my three men of many lessons, and they with me. We have simply moved away from each other and into different classrooms.

I now know that I am healed and healing, and in my own way perfect and imperfect all at once. Rather than wishing my scars away I see them and allow them to be. I surrendered the need to do the perfect job of grief and let my loss take a rest on the bench. Sure, some days I can do grief damn well, other days I suck at it. Ah well, so be it. I surrender.

The only way to get out of grief is to be the one who dies first. To be human is to love, and love opens us to the inevitability of loss and the grief that comes. And how do we hold these stories for each other, for ourselves? In truth, grief invites love stories, and love is on top of the list.

A Series of Surrenders

It may look to you like I am sad. I am.

It may look to you like my heart is breaking over and over. It is.

It may look to you that I repeat memories of old and tear up at moments that will never be. I do.

But what is it you do not see?

The invisible part of me, my soul, is in a fertile field of growth.

As I lean into new lessons in love my soul is stretching and expanding.

To miss so fully, to grieve so deeply, is a testament to the love that began many moons ago.
The love that never dies.
The love that delivers new layers of lessons.

So to you it may look like I am stuck. I am not. I am expanding.

Make space and look for layers you cannot see, for in the invisible is the magic.

Big Love,
Deb D

Acknowledgments and Thanks

CREATIVE TEAM

Ian William Brown, Editor & Writing Mentor
Ian, my longtime friend, and creative inspiration. Ian is the first writer I ever called my friend. Before I believed I could write, he was a writer. When I began to write this book he became my touchstone. I reached to Ian the first time I had a writer's question and a creative problem to solve. I knew Ian would know the answer, and he did. Ian has been generous and supportive of me as a writer, and more importantly, as a human working on managing an ever-changing heart. Ian was at the burial services of all three deaths that have shaped my life and he has stood by me in times of birth, death, and all the creation in between.

Liz Driscoll (LifaLif), Creative Consultant
When my little sister Elizabeth was born I fell in love in a way I never had before. I wished deeply that she was my child and cared for her as if she was. Watching Liz grow into the amazing woman she is, has been and is, one of my great joys in this life. This joy is deepened when she supports me with my dreams by adding her creative talents and shaping my ideas with her creative flair. As we grow together Liz and I will create more.

Steph Houle, Designer

Steph is a creative spirit that breathes imagination into life. She sees the world through a kaleidoscope of possibilities and the way she greets those she meets is with an open smile that invites you in. It is with this spirit that she approaches her design work, and thus, magic is made. https://stephaniehoule.com/

Deep Gratitude and BIG Love

Family and Friends

Many amazing people in my life have held my hand as I crafted this book. Thank you to everyone who listened as I shared the next stage of the book, asked me how the writing was progressing, and who shared their own memories that have shaped this narrative.

Gratitude and love to my mother, Barbara, my sisters, Kathy, Sandra, Judith, Heather, and Elizabeth.

To my soul sisters and brothers, I appreciate and love you.

Love and thanks to: Julie, Nina, Mardi, Kate, Justine, Shez, Hayley, Joh, Lucy, Krissy, Tammy, Sidd, Eduardo, Alexandra, Anna

To Smokey, thank you for loving me exactly as I am and in the way you do.

Many thanks to Elham, Elena and Kate for supporting my process by being the first to read the book and to offer insight and reflections.

Tobago, Caribbean Jewel, the island where this book was written.

In Tobago, I found my writing spot and a wide horizon with deep sunsets, rainbows, and pelicans.

On the last day of my first trip to Tobago, the owner of Miller's Guest House, my writing spot, said to me: "You smile more now than you did when you first arrived," and he is right. Since I met Tobago, her beaches, cliffs and oceans, her people and her blessings, I smile more.

Debra Lynne Driscoll

A Place for grieving hearts to land and souls to expand.

The message received in my dream by the guide, *'The research is important,'* has found ground and informs my act of service. My story is the launchpad for my work. Guided by Grief, my intuition, and the tools I have learned in my journey, I work with individuals and groups to help them to unwrap the gifts that death offers and to make friends with the grief that comes after a loved one has died, or life has delivered a loss.

My acts of service:

- Grief Guidance & Intuitive Mentoring. Online, in person guidance with Debra
- Your Love Story, a writing & healing group program
- Reiki Courses & Healings
- Oracle Card Guidance
- Speaking Engagements & Workshops

Connect with me at **www.debralynnedriscoll.com**

YOUR GRATITUDE GIFT

THANK YOU for sharing your time with me and my story.

My wish when writing the book was for my story to be a catalyst for reflection and learning.

My desire is to ignite curiosity into the readers' own journey with loss and to inspire the possibilities for healing the hurt and easing the ouch.

In service of this wish, and in gratitude, I have created a special gift for you.

Go to **debralynnedriscoll.com/a-series-of-surrenders-gift** to receive your free gift.

Big Love & Many Blessings,
Debra

CPSIA information can be obtained
at www.ICGtesting.com
Printed in the USA
LVHW090033140420
653355LV00004B/1338